RITA

HONORING HEROES OF A FORGOTTEN STORM

By Jane McBride

Edited by Beth Gallaspy

A Pediment Book

Jane McBride

Published by Pediment Publishing, a division of The Pediment Group, Inc. www.pediment.com Printed in Canada

Table of Contents

Dedication

This book is dedicated to the heroes of Hurricane
Rita: the first responders, elected officials, civic leaders, medical care providers, government employees, service organizations, faith-based teams, business owners, and others who answered the call to help those in need.

For each person whose role is mentioned in the book, there are a hundred more whose stories are not told, but whose contributions were significant and deserving of recognition.

Each citizen who emptied his or her neighbor's refrigerator, used a chain saw to clear roads and yards, took food and water to someone who was hungry and thirsty, donated money, volunteered countless hours in relief efforts, and participated in all the other ways in which neighbors take care of each other – these are the heroes of Hurricane Rita.

The nation quickly forgot Rita, but those whose lives you touched in ways both simple and profound never will forget you.

Each of you is a hero – and my hope is that this book does justice to your efforts.

Preface

The images of the monster storm brought terror to those whose lives lay in her path. With 175 mph winds, she was the third strongest storm on record in the Atlantic Basin. With frightening clarity, radar images captured the massive, swirling bands of a Category 5 hurricane that filled the entire Gulf of Mexico.

Those who watched the increasingly alarming television reports didn't have to wonder what this storm was capable of. Just three weeks earlier, they watched horrific images of bodies floating in the sewage-and-debris-filled waters Hurricane Katrina sent pouring through the neighborhoods of New Orleans and surrounding parishes.

They watched parents clutching babies in trees as currents pulled hungrily at them. They wept as they watched images of the most vulnerable of the city's citizens clinging to rooftops near holes they had hacked through attics in desperation.

Only someone living in complete isolation was unaware of Katrina. She captured the attention of a stunned nation as media from around the globe scrambled to tell her story. Dramatic coverage prompted financial support from government, celebrities, non-profits and ordinary Americans who pull together in a crisis.

Just 270 miles down Interstate 10 from New Orleans, Southeast Texans were among the first to welcome Katrina evacuees. They built a make-shift city inside the huge Ford Park Complex, where they housed, fed and clothed Louisianans. They provided phones, computers, medical and psychological support, all with city, county and state money, augmented by the generosity of non-profits, faith-based organizations, industry leaders and philanthropists.

First responders and volunteers worked tirelessly, spending 18-hour days tending to the evacuees' needs.

When it became obvious Hurricane Rita was headed to the Louisiana-Texas line, Southeast Texans had to relocate thousands of Katrina evacuees before they could even think about taking care of themselves. More than 3 million people would flee the storm, clogging the highways with the largest single evacuation in America's 229-year history.

Hurricane Rita blew ashore near Sabine Pass, wiping out entire coastal communities as she straddled the Texas/Louisiana line. Her winds ripped trees from the ground, hammering them through homes, businesses and across roads. She destroyed many hundreds of miles of power lines and disabled city infrastructures, leaving citizens without the most basic of needs – potable water, food sources, electricity, transportation, medical care and functioning sewer systems. In Louisiana, she swept entire cities inland, leaving a mass of broken structures, roads and lives.

During those first critical 72 hours in Southeast Texas, many of the state and national resources that were expected to show up to help were in short supply, if they showed up at all. Manpower and services were stretched to the breaking point, placed in and around New Orleans and west and south of where the storm finally hit.

Ambulances necessary to transport special needs patients were missing. Fuel supplies were so limited as to be useless. When generators finally arrived, they were such a valuable commodity that regional and federal government officials ended up in a face-off at Ford Park.

Officials at the emergency operations centers, plans in place, found themselves facing a situation no one could have foreseen. Emergency services contracts they relied on were pretty much useless; resources were tied up or stockpiled elsewhere.

In those first frightening hours and days after most of the populace left and Rita came ashore, it became clear that if anyone would help those in harm's way, it would be neighbors. Local and regional elected officials, emergency management coordinators, first responders, non-profit organizations, volunteers and faith-based teams all took extraordinary measures to protect and serve.

This is their story.

Chapter One

The Katrina Effect

Talking about Hurricane Rita is impossible without
first looking at Hurricane Katrina. When Katrina's category 3 storm
surge hit on August 29, 2005, she brought widespread damage to Southeast Louisiana and Mississippi. When the wall of water breeched the
levee in New Orleans, it flooded the city, which sits below sea level. The
shallow earthen bowl filled with sea water, sewage and other contami-
nants, covering entire neighborhoods. More than 1,800 people died, most
of them in Louisiana and Mississippi.

The National Hurricane Center and National Weather Service did
their job, tracking the monster storm and forecasting landfall in time for
those in the storm's path to evacuate. Still, the widespread poverty in
New Orleans, coupled with an inability to mobilize transportation to get
all the city's citizens out in time, resulted in thousands of people being
left behind. Many stayed by choice, only to realize too late the folly of
that decision. Others wanted to leave, but emptying a city the size of
New Orleans would take an untested, well-planned, well-orchestrated,
well-equipped effort. That didn't happen. Many of those in charge of
watching out for their citizens failed miserably.

When the hundreds of thousands of evacuees fled New Orleans ahead of – and after – Katrina, Beaumont, Texas, was one of their first stops along Interstate 10. Southeast Texas leaders, led by Jefferson County Judge Carl Griffith and emergency responders, turned the county's large Ford Park Complex into a makeshift city. The county bore the significant cost, without any assurance they would be reimbursed by the federal government.

Southeast Texans responded to the evacuees' plight in historic numbers. Non-profits, volunteer organizations, faith-based groups, medical personnel, mental health professionals and ordinary people showed up to see what they could do to help those who had been displaced. For three weeks, they worked around the clock, seven days a week, tending to the evacuees' needs. They set up phone and computer banks to help victims contact family members and apply for aid. They set up cots and shower facilities, opened a kitchen that provided three meals a day, organized massive amounts of donated clothing and supplies, brought in barbers and hair stylists, helped parents get their children temporarily enrolled in school, found jobs for those who wanted them, and did everything they could to make a horrible situation more bearable.

The demands were beyond anything workers had experienced before. By the time Hurricane Rita began her path toward the Gulf of Mexico, they were exhausted, both physically and mentally. Setting up Ford Park as a temporary shelter had been a huge undertaking. Emptying the park had been a massive challenge. First, transportation had to be secured to move the evacuees to shelters outside the storm's path. Paperwork to track the evacuees had to be completed and manifests made. They left on buses, planes, private car and ambulances, headed to cities all across the United States. It was a sloppy, confused endeavor, with no precedent on which to base plans. But they all got out.

When the Ford center was empty, volunteers faced a sickening sight. The huge facility was filled with garbage and medical waste. Workers had to clear away mounds of filthy debris and cast-off trash, then scrub the facility down before it could be used as an emergency staging center for the hurricane aiming straight for Southeast Texas.

For Southeast Texans, the Ford center was the hub for response to both of those horrible events in late summer 2005. For most of the nation, only one is remembered.

Ask any American across the country about the hurricanes of 2005 and they will remember Katrina. Rightly so; for those who lost homes, livelihoods and family members, it will go down as one of the dark times in American history.

Ask about Rita, and the response is entirely different. Rita was the forgotten storm. There were no horrifying video clips of Southeast Texans clinging to rooftops or trees as flood waters rushed just feet away. No images of dozens of desperate people lined up on a bridge waiting for someone – anyone – to take them out of harm's way.

For that, in part, Southeast Texans owe a debt to Katrina. She was a wake-up call that made formerly complacent folks aware of exactly how merciless a storm could be. They watched, and they learned. When officials called a mandatory evacuation for Rita, all those painful images of Katrina still were fresh. An unprecedented 3 million people heeded the warning in the largest evacuation ever in the United States, though the gridlock made it a horrific trip, especially for the elderly and ill, many of whose deaths would be hastened by the intense heat and stress. Though their numbers were not counted in the death toll, they lost their lives in the months after the storm, unable to recover from the trauma.

Those who bear responsibility for citizens under their care had raw memories of their own. They joined together in a single goal – to make sure what happened in New Orleans didn't happen in Southeast Texas and Southwest Louisiana.

The second storm caused much more damage than outsiders knew. The numbers help tell the story: 7,590 homes destroyed and 27,480 suffering major damage in 22 affected Texas counties; $35 million in damage to Lamar University in Beaumont; 62,000 claims to Texas Workforce; $3,749,698,351 in FEMA claims.

But numbers are a cold, inanimate summary that can't convey the suffering Southeast Texans and Southwest Louisianans endured from Katrina's all but ignored stepsister.

The one number that should stand out – the one Southeast Texans hold onto when they read stories and reports and watch national celebrity-studded fundraising efforts for Katrina – is the casualty count. Any loss of life is a tragedy; just ask the family members and friends of the five people who died of carbon monoxide poisoning after Rita. Ask those whose frail loved one's deaths were hastened by the evacuation.

In a bitter irony, the low loss of life kept attention and support away from Rita's victims. No one stopped to ask why so few perished because of the storm.

Loosely defined, Southeast Texas consists of six counties. Much of the area, especially the counties to the north and east that form the outer edges of East Texas, is heavily forested; at one time, sawmills sprung up in communities all across the area. Beaumont, Port Arthur and Orange, the three largest cities in the region, each have a deep-water port. Southeast Texas is home to multiple petrochemical plants and industry that supply a huge chunk of the nation's oil, gas and related products.

Lakes, rivers, bays, bayous and the Gulf of Mexico provide ample opportunities for outdoor activities and put succulent seafood on tables. Some form of shrimp, oysters, fish and crawfish can be found on the menu at most restaurants.

The proximity to all that water contributes to the area's economy and recreational enjoyment. But sitting along the Gulf of Mexico has a price, and it's a steep one.

In "The Great Storm" of September 8, 1900, a hurricane packing winds at an estimated 140 mph blasted across Galveston Island, a resort community south of Houston. At the time of the storm, the highest elevation in Galveston was 8.7 feet. The storm surge topped 15.7 feet. The churning waters destroyed buildings and picked up everything in its path, using the debris to further push inland. An unaware population had no place to hide as the muddy waters covered the island. At least 6,000 to 8,000 of the city's 37,000 residents died. More than 3,600 buildings were obliterated.

The 1900 Storm was the deadliest natural disaster in U.S. history. To protect the island against future hurricanes, the city built a seawall and literally raised the island by eight to 10 feet. Though the seawall, which sits 15.6 feet above sea level, helps protect the city, it cannot handle major hurricanes. Three years after Rita, Hurricane Ike would leave flood waters 4 feet deep and more in some areas of Galveston.

Port Arthur is even more vulnerable and less protected from a strong storm surge. At a mere 7 feet above sea level, its vulnerability prompted the construction of a seawall completed in 1984. The seawall protects Groves, Port Neches, Nederland and Port Arthur, including refineries. The wall was designed to protect against a storm surge of 15 feet. During Hurricane Ike in 2008, the water was mere inches from overtaking the wall.

The statistics, as clear as they are, don't seem enough to adequately convey just how much at risk the area is. History has shown that the general public tends to dismiss the possibility of a disaster that would result in catastrophic loss of life and property.

Emergency responders, political leaders and industry officials found everything they thought they knew about preparing for a disaster put to the test as they responded to Hurricane Rita.

Chapter Two

Ford Park

As a fifth-generation Texan from a ranching back- ground, Carl Griffith believed he was destined to help shape the future of the county he'd lived in all his life, as had his father and grandfather. By age 10, the sandy-haired boy had decided that one day he would be the sheriff of Jefferson County. Unlike most kids, whose answer to "what do you want to be when you grow up" changes with the wind, he never swayed from his goal.

Griffith earned an associate degree in police science and a bachelor's in criminal justice, then went on to earn a master's degree in education with an emphasis on counseling.

In 1988, he made his first bid, running for sheriff against an incumbent who had held the job for 26 years. Griffith ran on a platform of reform that included raising the standards for department hires and creating a more professional staff. Under their new sheriff, officers were required to have at least 60 college hours. Those who didn't had to commit to completing those hours within three years. During his eight years as sheriff, Griffith began developing a leadership style that would be tested and refined, but like his childhood ambition, never abandoned.

In 1997, he ran for and was elected Jefferson County Judge, where he developed a reputation for being decisive and tenacious. As a politician, he began forging friendships and working relationships that included a future president, senators, congressmen and a governor or two. All those relationships would be needed when two closely spaced hurricanes put Southeast Texas to the test.

During his 10 years as county judge, Griffith and a team of forward-looking civic leaders courted industry leaders, offering tax incentives that brought in more than $13 billion in commercial and industrial expansion projects.

Griffith's ambitious plans to grow the county and make it not only rich in industry and business, but also as an entertainment destination earned him many friends and supporters. It also drew the ire of detractors who didn't agree with his progressive style, especially when it came to anything that would raises taxes.

In 2001, he began pursuing an ambitious plan to bring a major entertainment complex to Southeast Texas. In 2002, with the support of the Commissioners Court, he secured a deal for a park that included a 9,737-seat arena, an 83,000 square-foot exhibit hall, 12 sports fields used for fast-pitch softball and youth baseball competitions, a nine-acre midway home to the South Texas State Fair and an outdoor concert and entertainment pavilion that seats 18,000. The complex also has an RV park, the Ben Rogers Regional Visitors Center and eight meeting rooms.

Griffith secured a national sponsor who paid a premium for naming rights. The complex became Ford Park, named after the auto giant.

Although the Commissioners Court backed the plan, Griffith was the one who took the heat for making the deal without putting the county-taxpayer supported center to a public referendum, especially after cost overruns increased the original budget. A complicated set of circumstances, including a downturn in the entertainment business, poor management at the park and weak ticket sales, along with a weakening economy in general, would make it hard for the county to keep its promise that the complex wouldn't result in a tax hike.

By August 2005, the personable civic leader who had never lost an election was facing public criticism and a challenger for the office.

When Jack Colley, head of the DPS Texas Division of Emergency Management, called Griffith and said he desperately needed help finding places that could temporarily house the thousands of evacuees fleeing Louisiana after Hurricane Katrina hit, the judge immediately thought of the big complex. Ford Park, once considered his political problem, became the first shelter to be set up in Texas.

Griffith went to work calling all the mayors in the county, along with other leaders who promised to send staff to help.

He asked Jefferson County Emergency Management Coordinator John Cascio to call in emergency managers from around the county. The largest contingent came from Port Arthur and Mid-County, though all the managers provided help. County Commissioner Everett "Bo" Alfred enlisted the Jefferson County Health Department, and Ingrid Homes brought in the City of Beaumont's Health Department to provide medical care. Linda Turk of the Texas Workforce Development Board offered invaluable support in providing staff to screen the evacuees for services.

More than 27,000 evacuees would pass through Ford Park in the next three weeks. Many stayed until forced to find housing. Others moved on after getting help. At any given time, the shelter occupancy averaged around 3,000 people. It was a massive undertaking, with thousands of cots placed side with side, affording no privacy to evacuees. Hundreds of volunteers aided the Salvation Army, American Red Cross and other non-profits and charities in collecting, sorting and distributing clothing, formula, personal toiletries and other needs, as well as cooking and feeding evacuees. Ford Park became a small city, with temporary shower facilities, first aid stations, computer and phone centers and more.

Among the core group of professionals to augment Griffith's leadership was Brit Featherston, an Assistant U.S. Attorney for the Eastern District of Texas. Featherston was born and raised in Port Arthur, where he began his law enforcement career as a police officer in 1981. Featherston left the department nine years later to go to law school in Waco, only to realize how much he missed law enforcement. He joined the district attorney's office in Brazoria County, and then later applied to the U.S. Attorney's Office. He was hired and began work at the office in Lufkin in 1996.

Featherston's career put him in the path of several disasters, developing the skills he would need when Griffith called him in after Hurricane Katrina hit.

In 2001, he took a position with the U.S. Justice Department in Washington, D.C. He was serving there on September 11, when terrorists flew a plane into the Pentagon.

Featherston moved his family back to Texas in 2003, serving in the Lufkin office, which was the anti-terrorism headquarters for the district. Featherston worked there on "anything involving terrorism threats and anti-terrorism efforts, working with refineries, the U.S. Coast Guard, law enforcement, critical infrastructure and anything concerning it and aiding local law enforcement agencies."

He worked the Columbia Space Shuttle Disaster in 2003. The shuttle exploded 200,000 feet above the earth, scattering thousands of pieces of debris in a 150-mile-long path, much of it centered in the Lufkin and Nacogdoches area. Featherston worked with the FBI setting up the command center for the recovery, which called in FEMA and NASA.

Featherston left Lufkin in May 2005, just in time to become involved in the next disaster, one that hit much closer to home.

As crisis management coordination and district supervisor for the Beaumont Division of the U.S. Attorney's Office, a large part of his responsibility was making sure the office could function no matter what the circumstances.

The U.S. Attorney's office probably is not the first agency that comes to mind during a hurricane, Featherston noted in the diary he kept during his 2005 hurricane experience.

"Just what does the U.S. Attorney's Office contribute to a command center (like Ford Park) during an event like Katrina? No community has a group of people on standby to work in a command post that coordinates the feeding, medical, sleeping, and education needs of 1,700 men, women and children who, in a matter of hours, lost every material possession they owned," he wrote.

"It was a feat too large for just the Red Cross or Salvation Army. The tenure of the crisis lasted much longer than the attention of the most well-intentioned, but fleeting, local volunteers," he said. "That left police and fire personnel who were assigned to handle all those issues as well as tending to their day jobs. The crisis required people to step in and give their time (18 hour days) to making decisions in the interest of the evacuees and, as well, in the interest of the community that was footing the bill."

"We negotiated contracts for trash service. You would not believe the size of the trash pile that accumulates during an event like this.

"We decided when to remove individuals from the population due to the suspicion of theft from volunteers (at Ford Park).

"We developed ideas and solutions on how to disperse 300, $100 gift cards to over 1,000 individuals who began arriving at the park hours before the cards were going to be given out, and stood in line in 100 degree heat.

"We assisted law enforcement in seeking out fabricators making claims for money and goods that were not deserving of the charity.

"We understood the reason and had the necessary skill to assist in public service announcements to keep the public aware of what was going on in their community.

"We acted as the spokesperson between Beaumont and the state command center.

"And finally, we made decisions like locking the rear doors of the complex because there had been too much criminal mischief to county property.

"We did a good job," he noted, "and finally, all of the evacuees were gone."

Two days later, an exhausted Featherston would be back on the job for Rita, along with Robert Hobbs, who worked with Featherston in the U.S. Attorney's Office. Hobbs' and Featherston's relationship went back to the days when both were police officers. Featherston had worked for the Port Arthur Police Department while Hobbs worked with county law enforcement alongside Griffith, a deputy at the time. He later worked for Griffith when he was elected Sheriff of Jefferson County. It was at Griffith's request that Orwig released the pair to work with Griffith during Rita preparation and recovery.

As Katrina evacuees began filling Ford Park, leaders throughout the region began evaluating their own emergency response plans in case Southeast Texas faced a hurricane in the remaining months of the season. Griffith turned to key personnel in nearby cities as partners in refining the county's plan.

When it comes to experience and training, few exceed John Owens and Steve Curran, two career public servants who forged a professional and personal friendship through a shared sense of responsibility.

Deputy Chief of Police John Owens had been a deputy chief since 1999 and second in command at the Port Arthur Police Department since 2005. He had served as the city's emergency management coordinator for four years when Rita put his team to the test.

Steve Curran had served in the Port Arthur Fire Department for almost 29 years. He spent 16 of those as second in command (Fire Marshal and Deputy Chief) and 18 months as chief before retiring and taking the job as fire chief and emergency management coordinator for the smaller nearby City of Port Neches. Curran and Owens developed an emergency evacuation plan, teaming with emergency management coordinators from the four cities in South and Mid-Jefferson County: Port Arthur, Groves, Nederland and Port Neches.

Owens, Curran, and Groves Fire Chief Dale Jackson believed the cities' emergency responders and leaders needed to find a safe place to evacuate out of the storm surge zone. All four low-lying cities were vulnerable to flooding.

After Port Arthur Mayor Oscar Ortiz appointed him as emergency coordinator, Owens studied the city's emergency plans, looking for gaps and weaknesses. He found both. One of the biggest problems was the lack of a designated emergency operations center outside the flood area.

"I knew we were not going to be able to stay in Port Arthur if there was a substantial storm surge event. We needed a place close enough for a quick re-entry but out of the surge zone," Owens said.

They chose Lumberton, a small town of 8,700 about 10 miles north of Beaumont in nearby Hardin County.

The group met with Lumberton's chief of police, fire department chief, city manager and mayor, as well as the Lumberton Independent School District board. Lumberton agreed to make the high school and intermediate school available for first responders during a hurricane evacuation. They also would provide buses when needed for evacuation or other emergency transportation needs.

"Police Chief Norman Reynolds was very open to the idea, as were officials with the school district. Hardin County Judge Billy Caraway was very positive and open to our request," Owens said. "It was an unbelievable gesture of friendship to allow us to occupy their facility."

In a fortuitous stroke of timing prior to the 2005 hurricane season, the respective city and school attorneys drew up a memorandum of understanding. The emergency management teams devised a detailed and precise map of the school facilities and grounds. Each of the participating cities had its own area, but shared the same facility. The close proximity allowed maximum communication.

"We literally mapped out where each city would stay inside the school, as well as how we would feed our people and sustain any long-term occupation of that facility. We were able to get all that approved and blessed by not only the school district and City of Lumberton but also our city officials in Mid-and South County," Owens said.

Owens and Curran believed it was critical to include the area's industry leaders, primarily the petrochemical partners who were among the area's largest employers: Motiva, Valero, TOTAL, ExxonMobil, BASF-

FINA and Chevron-Phillips.

"They are not only stakeholders in our community, but are vital to our safety and well being once the storm has passed," Owens said.

With major refineries clustered in Southeast Texas, the area is extremely vulnerable to toxic chemical spills or leaks during an emergency, whether natural or man- made. During a hurricane, when a timely response is critical to safeguarding the public, the presence of key petro-chemical leaders is vital.

"With these facilities and their susceptibility to hazardous substances releases, we wanted to ensure we had the decision makers there with us in Lumberton," Owens said.

The timing of the plan couldn't have been better. The day the first evacuees from Hurricane Katrina began streaming into Jefferson County, Owens and Curran were meeting with Reynolds, Lumberton's emergency management coordinator, to finalize and sign off on the emergency evacuation plan.

A key element of the plan was the signing of interlocal agreements with 23 industry partners prior to Hurricane Katrina. Interlocal agreements permit a local government to enter into specified agreements with other entities to cooperatively share resources for their mutual benefit, especially during a time of emergency. Those agreements would be critical during a hurricane, when immediate access to equipment and other resources can be severely limited.

"We were ahead of the curve on that, ahead of the rest of the county," Curran said. "Every detail was all laid out."

Owens and Curran were on their way back home from Lumberton when they received a call from Roy Birdsong of the Jefferson County Sheriff's Department, asking them to come to Ford Park to help with the influx of evacuees from Louisiana, including a small group of gang members.

"We got there and they had no real help," Curran said. "Judge Carl Griffith grabbed Chief Owens and me and said 'Y'all can't leave. I'm calling your mayor. What do I need to do to keep you here?' We basically set up the emergency operations center there."

Curran and Owens both are members of the Sabine Neches Chiefs Association, a group of public and private entities who share information and resources focused on preparedness, prevention, response and recovery after emergencies or disasters. Those contacts means he knows "where all the stuff is," Curran said. Owens currently is president of the group.

"We started getting the resources there. We even got a local plumbers union to build makeshift showers. We just got real creative and started building a mini-city. We processed over 27,000 evacuees through Ford Park. We maintained and kept close to 4,000 to 5,000 evacuees at any given time. They were coming in and out," Curran said.

In an evacuee camp as large as the one at Ford Park, medical care poses a special problem. Physicians, nurses and other medical staff have to be pulled from their regular duties to become medical providers.

From the county standpoint, the primary responsibility falls on Dr. Cecil Walkes, Director of the Jefferson County Health Department. The small department has a staff of 26; only six of those are nurses. Caring for the needs of the citizens of the county keeps them busy during normal times. When Katrina evacuees filled Ford Park, Walkes had to find a way to provide care for those with both acute and chronic conditions.

Katrina provided a wakeup call that the county hadn't experienced in many years, Walkes said. The county set up field stations at Ford Park to screen people for immediate and after-care. Some area physicians volunteered their time at the park, augmenting the county and city staff.

Walkes called a close friend who works in the White House, asking for help, and Washington sent a Disaster Medical Assistance Team (DMAT) from California.

DMAT teams are professional and para-professional medical personnel who provide medical care during disasters. The teams augment local medical professionals during the gap from the time of the event until the federal government can step in. They are self-sustaining, bringing in their own equipment and supplies for the two weeks they are deployed.

The California team included a physician, three nurses, a health specialist and a pharmacist. Walkes and his team met with the DMAT team to assess problems they encountered during Katrina so they could make appropriate changes before the next storm. Of course, they didn't know that would be less than a month away. By that time, the DMAT team had left.

"Rita came on the heels of Katrina so quickly we didn't have time to digest all of those problems," Walkes said. "But at least we had a taste of what could occur, and we were a bit more prepared for it."

The single biggest lesson learned was the importance of medical records. Walkes and his team were being asked to treat patients without any idea of what their existing medical conditions were or what medications they were taking. Most of the patients couldn't provide a history. Some patients needed dialysis; others were HIV positive and without any meds.

"We learned that people should have some basic knowledge of their history to take with them wherever they were sent, because we had so many of those people without anything and we didn't have anyone to call. At that point, you just have to assess the patient yourself and prescribe according to your findings."

Port Arthur, the second largest city in Jefferson County, sent the city's Human Resources Director Dr. Al Thigpen and his assistant, H.R. Analyst Cheryl Gibbs to Ford Park to manage finances for the care of Katrina evacuees. That included finding housing for families, arranging transportation to get them to their next destination and running the financial distribution center for gift cards donated by charitable organizations.

Ford Park was intended to be a temporary shelter to help relocate Katrina evacuees to other parts of the country, but day after day passed with few leaving and many more coming through. It quickly became obvious that many of the evacuees didn't understand that New Orleans would not be coming back any time soon, and they would need to find another place to live.

"I'm sure they were depressed over everything they had experienced and weren't focused on looking for a place to stay," Griffith said.

The county set a deadline for evacuees to move to state and federally supported locations, making announcements each day. FEMA provided funds for housing so they could make more permanent plans. The county arranged for transportation.

On the day before the deadline, a community in North Texas offered apartments. The state sent buses to Ford Park to pick up the last of the evacuees on Friday, a week before Rita made landfall and two days before emergency management began gearing up for Rita.

By then, the temporary plan had stretched out for three weeks, exhausting the people working around the clock and the resources designated for relief.

"Judge Griffith had to deal with the pressure of the evacuees coming through the county and getting them moved on, then had to deal with Jefferson County and the widespread devastation we had. This happened at a time when, from an emergency management viewpoint, the country's resources were strained. There had been significant flooding in the Midwest, wildfires on the West Coast and then Hurricane Katrina," Thigpen said.

Few people were more aware of the strain on the federal government that year than Tammy Doherty, a regional deputy director for FEMA who was sent to Beaumont a few days after Hurricane Katrina. It was an unusual move, but necessary because FEMA's coordinating officers were stretched so thin.

"As a deputy director on a regional level we typically weren't ones to work disasters. But in years when there was way too much going on they would collar some of us," said Doherty, who was based in FEMA's Region 10 office, covering Washington State, Oregon, Idaho and Alaska. She had worked several disasters before she was promoted, including a lower-level hurricane in Louisiana.

By the time Doherty arrived at Ford Park, other FEMA individual assistance staff already had set up an office to assist the public.

"I think it was furnished by the City of Beaumont, because we didn't have anything with us," Doherty said. "We ended up bringing in a few other people we needed, like a congressional liaison to do public affairs."

The FEMA crew outgrew the Ford Park office just about the time Judge Griffith was trying to move out the last of the evacuees. He asked FEMA to find another location. The logistics staff at FEMA headquarters arranged contracts for a new office in Beaumont, including fully furnishing the space.

"Everything was going fine at that point. Everything that we were using at the Ford center had been furnished for us. We weren't taking our computers or printers or anything. The logistics contractor was supposed to have everything in the building," Doherty said.

Doherty had issued press releases and published notices in the local newspapers telling people where to go and on what date to apply for federal assistance after Katrina. The day before the opening, the logistics contractor threatened to pull out.

"I was notified that this guy was going somewhere else. There were several victim centers set up in Texas. One was at the Houston Astrodome and one in San Antonio. Somehow he thought it was more important to send it there than honoring his contract in Beaumont."

Doherty called Griffith, who offered to go with her to confront the contractor.

"We went down there with the intention of telling him, 'You have to do this. We have to have this equipment.' I think had Judge Griffith not been there, I would not have been able to convince him. The judge really strong-armed the guy, who ended up saying 'OK, we'll set it up.' We had to work all night, but we were able to get the office opened the next morning."

The logistics contractor left for another location and sent someone new in his place, which was good news for Doherty.

"The guy he brought in was much easier to deal with. The first guy was just a real pain in the ass."

Doherty was impressed by the willingness of the county to take on such a huge project as turning Ford Park into a shelter. At that point, county officials didn't have any idea whether they would be reimbursed for the costs they incurred, Doherty said.

"The same thing was true for Houston and other places that housed evacuees. They had done it because there was a need for it, but there was no legal way to reimburse anybody. I'm assuming the City of Beaumont or Jefferson County just said. 'OK we'll figure out reimbursement later.' They had a lot of expenses. During the conference calls we had every day we would talk about those kinds of issues."

Griffith said that was indeed the case.

"We weren't sure we would get reimbursed. It was completely up in the air. But I made the decision to go ahead and make Ford Park available."

Closing Ford Park as a shelter on Friday, Sept. 16 became critical to the future of Jefferson County and surrounding areas. By then, the remnants of an old front and a tropical wave had merged into an "area of disturbed weather." By the next evening, it was a tropical depression. On Sunday, it became a tropical storm.

Everyone with a role in protecting the citizens of Southeast Texas went on alert at the news that this storm was moving toward the warm waters of the Gulf, pulling energy from the sea to feed its hunger.

While Hurricane Katrina evacuees were headed out, Rita was heading in. Once she entered the Gulf of Mexico, Rita would swell from a Category 2 to a Category 5 hurricane in less than 24 hours.

Chapter Three

Storm Preparations

By 2005, Greg Bostwick had spent 32 years studying weather patterns and perfecting the science of forecasting under imperfect conditions. As the chief meteorologist for KFDM-TV Channel 6 in Beaumont, he built a solid reputation as a dependable weather source.

When a hurricane threatens, meteorologists become invaluable. Bostwick, a no-nonsense Texas A&M grad who takes his role seriously, has little use for scaremongers. For him, it's an opportunity to promote professionalism, not panic.

"My philosophy is not to sensationalize it. If it is a threat, say it is, but don't make every storm that comes down the pike a disaster. I believe if you cry wolf enough, you won't have the response you want when the storm comes."

Bostwick is confident of his skills and the role he plays during a severe weather event, but he has no illusions about the fleeting attention that comes with the territory.

"It's an interesting thing; when you are a meteorologist covering a hurricane, you are the alpha dog when the storm is coming. You are the one dominating the newscast. They are telling the poor sports guys, OK, you can take a few days off. We don't need to talk about sports right now."

"But it's one of these weird deals. Before the storm, you are at the apex of Mount Everest. After the storm hits and moves on, you drop to Death Valley. You go from the heights to the depths in just a matter of hours. I went from doing wall-to-wall weather to almost no weather in the aftermath. There is an adrenalin rush, then a collapse of emotions when it's over. We still did weathercasts – but mainly on how it was going to affect recovery."

Bostwick is a sought-after speaker for refineries, civic groups, clubs and schools. Unlike his television and radio forecasts, where the only people in the room are Bostwick, a camera and crew, speaking engagements let him gauge the public's response.

"You see their faces and you see immediately if you are making an impression. In all the years before Rita, I got the impression people thought, yeah, hurricanes are a threat but they don't come here. As if we had a force field that keeps storms away," he laughed. "There was a thought process that a hurricane may threaten us, but it will turn and hit somebody else. When they saw the maps of Rita coming toward us, it started shaking people up. They started thinking, 'Maybe this is one we're not going to dodge.'"

All Bostwick had to do to bring the message home was stress the strength of the monster storm bearing down on Southeast Texas.

"The gold standard for measuring a storm is the lower the pressure, the worse the storm. Rita had a lower pressure than Katrina and the Air Force reconnaissance plane measured stronger winds than Katrina had. We said that, knowing full well people were still seeing images from Katrina and New Orleans. We didn't have any trouble getting people's attention."

Bostwick knows that among those who stay closely tuned to his forecasts are the people who have to assess the danger to their communities. Foremost are the ones who have to make the call to shelter in place – or evacuate.

Guy Goodson had been sitting in the mayor's chair for barely four months when his city faced the largest disaster in Beaumont's history. He wasn't new to public service; he'd served on the city council for six terms from 1990 to 2003 before leaving to focus on his law career. He decided to run for mayor in 2004.

Goodson took the oath of office in May 2005. Over the Fourth of July holiday he took home two large three-ring binders that detailed the city's emergency management manuals, almost on a lark, he said. He studied his responsibilities carefully but gave only a cursory review to the rest of the plan.

Six weeks later Hurricane Katrina hit Louisiana and Mississippi and hundreds of thousands of evacuees, primarily from the Greater New Orleans area, passed through Beaumont. A month after that, Rita came calling.

As mayor, the responsibility for Beaumont rested on his shoulders – and whether to call a mandatory evacuation was by far the most difficult decision he would make. The stakes were enormous. If he ordered the evacuation, it would effectively shut the city down. Literally every one of the city's 120,000 residents had something at stake.

Evacuating meant citizens would have to come up with money for gas, food and water for the trip. They would need a place to stay, which could mean substantial additional costs. Children, elderly parents and grandparents would need to be taken to safety. Pets presented another problem. Would they go with the family, be boarded in a kennel, or left at home defenseless?

For many folks, leaving town meant lost days of work without any assurance of compensation. For businesses, the lost revenue could mean the difference between a profit or loss for a month, at minimum. For some, it turned what would have been a profitable year into a loss. For major industries, it could mean the loss of millions of dollars in revenue.

Goodson hadn't forgotten what he had seen at Ford Park during the Katrina evacuation when his city workers became emotionally involved as they provided support for the evacuees.

"You hear about a fire in California or a tornado in the Midwest and you feel for those people, but it is intangible," he said. "With Katrina evacuees, there was a sense of loss you couldn't put your arms around. The evacuees knew the level of devastation but also knew that there wasn't much they could do about it – and they didn't feel the government was doing much about it either. People left New Orleans with a great foreboding about what they would find once they got back. I don't think anybody who worked with the evacuees would say it didn't have a dramatic effect on them."

As an elected official, Goodson was disturbed by the lack of cohesiveness among Louisiana's leaders during Katrina.

"I don't think any of us would not say it had a profound effect on us as we moved forward just a little over three weeks later. We were highly sensitized and on a higher state of readiness because of Katrina. It was a fairly good template for others to see how not to let things devolve," Goodson said.

Goodson knew he would be second-guessed on the evacuation of his citizens. Around him, other mayors were facing the same situation. They constantly kept an eye on the weather forecast, turning to the National Hurricane Center, the National Weather Service in Lake Charles and meteorologists like Bostwick for updates.

Goodson had joined emergency management teams during the twice daily briefings at the county's Emergency Operations Center (EOC) at the U.S. Coast Guard facility in Port Arthur. Listening to Bostwick's predictions heightened his awareness of just how much was at stake.

"At one point Rita had sustained winds at 165 and gusts at 180. If she had made landfall at that rate, based on historic records, it would have been like the storm that hit Galveston," Goodson said. "It was a very powerful, fast-moving storm that we could see as possibly being worse than Katrina. That boggled the mind."

During the briefing on Wednesday, the mayors and county judges agreed they had to make a decision and make it fast. The hurricane was projected to hit south of Galveston on Saturday.

Because of a hurricane's counter clockwise movement, the heaviest bands of wind and rain form on the east side of the eye. That put the Golden Triangle cities of Beaumont, Port Arthur and Orange on the "dirty side," which has the highest concentration of rain, winds and possibility of tornadoes and storm surge.

The group of city and county officials made the decision to call for the evacuation starting early Thursday morning. That would give evacuees 36 hours to get out of harm's way. Once the decision had been made, the mayors stepped back and turned to their emergency managers to implement plans.

"As mayor my main job prior to the storm was to make sure we managed resources and followed the plan. I was there to put a face on the storm and let people who were trained in a specialized area do their job – and not interfere with the proper conduct of emergency management," Goodson said.

"Judge Griffith had a much larger mission. He had the entire county to deal with. He's got to coordinate with mayors and chief executive officers. Carl gave a herculean effort working with Kay Bailey Hutchison and the feds to get those medical evacuations planes out before the hurricane. That was just an outstanding effort. I don't know how he wasn't just mentally and physically exhausted before the storm ever made landfall. The saving of lives cannot be adequately estimated, but I think he sleeps well at night. That effort they were able to put together was a feather in his cap and for the county. He was in a major coordinating role between state, federal and local assets, down there every day making sure the resources would continue to come in and out while we took care of specific problems."

By 9 a.m. Thursday, traffic already had slowed to a crawl. Goodson and Beaumont City Manager Kyle Hayes were working their way through Beaumont after driving by ExxonMobil to see if the huge refinery was shutting down. Their path took them by the Port of Beaumont, the fourth busiest port in the United States, as well as the busiest military port in the U.S. and the second busiest military port in the world. The port handles more than 120 million tons of cargo each year.

Goodson had played a key role in helping secure two of the port's most valuable assets, the Cape Vincent and the Cape Victory, cargo ships docked at the port as part of the Ready Reserve Fleet through a contract with the Maritime Administration. As attorney for the port, Goodson was intimately familiar with the operations there.

Goodson likes to say many of his successes come more from being as "lucky as the devil." Sometimes, he says, "Providence does wonderful things for you."

As he and Hayes drove by the port, Goodson saw a possible solution to one of the major problems the city was dealing with as part of the evacuation plan.

When a hurricane threatens a city, one of the logistical nightmares is finding a safe place to store critical equipment, from fire trucks and police cars to bulldozers and other heavy equipment. All are needed to get the infrastructure of a city back in operation once the storm has cleared.

After Hurricane Katrina, relief efforts in New Orleans were hampered by the dearth of available emergency vehicles because most had been flooded by the same waters plaguing residents.

Facing Rita, Beaumont officials initially looked at sending its emergency vehicles and heavy equipment to Hardin County, but were concerned about the intensity of the storm and the lack of an open place in the heavily forested county.

"We were going to move all of our emergency and heavy equipment up to Huntsville as part of the plan adopted before I became mayor,"

Goodson said. "Judge Griffith had begun taking to his judge friends as far away as Walker County. We were in the process of deciding where we were going to put all that equipment."

When Goodson approached the port, he glanced at the huge piece of equipment being used to tighten the lines on the ship. Goodson told Hayes to slow down so he could get a better look.

"The Cape Victory and Cape Vincent are like all ships of that size. They are designed to be at sea during a hurricane. You don't want them tied up because there is a greater likelihood of them being damaged at the dock than there is at sea. All of a sudden, it hit me. They are not leaving. They are lashing those ships down."

Hayes pulled into the port so Goodson could speak to the guard. Indeed, he learned, the ships were not leaving and had two tugboats scheduled to come in to hold them in place during the storm. Because they are roll on-roll off ships, both have massive gangways so the military can drive equipment in to be shipped to operations around the world, especially the Middle East. Both of the gangways still were down.

"I looked at Kyle and he looked at me and it's like we both realized that suddenly there was a perfect answer to an unsolvable problem. We could put all this equipment on the ships. The other great part of it is when we move our equipment so far away; it's hard to get it back through damaged areas. How do you remobilize in a hurry? Part of the problem with New Orleans was they lost so much equipment that was underwater they couldn't remobilize."

That was an immediate concern for Rita, a storm that, at the time, was intense enough to generate a projected 20 to 25-foot storm surge.

Goodson and Hayes met with Cape Vincent Master Capt. David Scott.

"I said, Dave, we have a strange request. You aren't leaving are you? He said, 'No'. I said, what would it take for us to be able to load all the fire and police and EMS vehicles on the ships? He said, 'Let's see what we can do.' There was never any hesitation. He got someone on the phone from Keystone Shipping in New Orleans and told them what we were up against. We got a telex back in less than two hours from the Maritime Administration saying that the City and other entities would have 'temporary but indeterminate use' of the Victory and Vincent for mobilization of these assets. Kyle starts calling and I start calling and within a matter of hours, we were putting equipment on the ships."

The agreement allowed Southeast Texas personnel to move 172

vehicles onto the Cape Vincent and 207 vehicles onto the Cape Victory, including fire trucks, ambulances, police vehicles and heavy equipment. Emergency responders and 30 rescue dogs also boarded the ship.

On the drive that led them to the port, Goodson had good reason to wonder if ExxonMobil was shutting down. The petroleum industry is one of the largest contributors to the economy in Southeast Texas. In refining oil and producing chemicals, the region's plants store and distribute a volatile mix of toxic chemicals and compounds.

ExxonMobil's chemical and lube plants sit on 2,400 acres near downtown Beaumont. The refinery opened in 1908, seven years after the Spindletop Gusher blew in, creating a population explosion and the beginning of the oil industry in the area. ExxonMobil employs around 2,000 workers, plus an additional 1,000 contractors. It processes 365,000 barrels of crude oil a day and produces 2.8 billion gallons of gasoline a year. It also has a polyprophelene plant (established in 1977) on 300 acres west of Beaumont near Highway 90.

During his term as mayor, Goodson had developed a strong working relationship with the key leaders of area refineries, including Lori Ryerkerk.

Ryerkerk had become the refinery's manager In March 2003. She quickly developed a reputation as an impeccable professional with a thorough knowledge of the petrochemical industry. Her outgoing personality, substantial intellect and sharp wit, as well as her commitment of financial support of area charities, earned her the respect of the community and the friendship of its leaders.

Watching her sister refinery in Chalmette, La. endure Hurricane Katrina intensified Ryerkerk's awareness of the criticalness of the plant's extensive and detailed emergency response plan. Their revised plan stated that if a mandatory evacuation was issued, 10 key workers would ride out the storm in the plant's explosion-proof building, which was stocked with a generator, food, water, gas masks and other emergency equipment, including a boat in case of flooding. They would be there to cope with any damage to the plant.

Ryerkerk's management team of 22 decided to ride out the storm at their polyprophelene plant west of Beaumont on Hwy 90, which sits on higher ground. After emptying the refinery, the staffers went by to check their homes before heading west.

Ryerkerk wasn't afraid for her personal safety. She was far more concerned about making the decision to shut the plant down.

"There is no worse feeling for a plant manager," she said. "It's the only time a plant has dead silence. There wasn't even any steam hissing. It's a very eerie feeling."

Ryerkerk's husband worked at ExxonMobil's chemical plant. She knew one of them would need to take their two children to a safe location out of the path of the storm. Because the refinery is more critical, Ryerkerk and her husband agreed he would take the children and she would stay to assess any damage and get the refinery up and running as quickly as possible.

She was the last person to leave the refinery, locking the gate behind her.

"I knew there was a possibility I'd made a $20 million mistake and could be criticized for being too cautious, but I couldn't take that chance. It would put too many people in the refinery at risk, plus the community," she said. "We wanted everyone to evacuate with their families."

Executives at the plants and refineries in South and Mid-County faced similar decisions.

TOTAL Human Resources and Communications Manager Pat Avery and Materials and Services Supervisor Randy Sonnier were among a "ride-out" team of seven designated to prepare their Port Arthur refinery for a hurricane.

TOTAL, which began refining in Port Arthur in 1936, has a capacity of 174,000 barrels a day of transportation fuels, petcoke, aromatics and liquefied petroleum gas. Most of the refinery's products are shipped across the country through pipelines.

The refinery's plan kicks into place when a storm enters the Gulf, at least 92 hours out from projected landfall, Avery said.

"When the county calls for an evacuation, we follow that to get most of our (600) employees out. We shut down and evacuate in stages. Operators can't leave until they shut the facility down safely," Sonnier said. "We are the ones who disconnect from the electrical grid and lock the gate – making us the last to leave. We turn the lights off, and we are gone."

Valero sits on 4,000 acres along the Port Arthur Ship Channel. The 800-employee refinery processes up to 310,000 barrels of crude oil per day, turning it into gasoline, diesel, jet fuel, petrochemicals, petroleum coke and sulfur. It also distributes products by pipeline.

Jim Gillingham had taken the top job as manager of the refinery on September 1 when Valero took over from previous owner Premcor.

Twenty-one days later, he was facing a hurricane.

Facing a possible storm surge that could inundate the refinery, the decision was made to shut the refinery down and evacuate personnel for the first time in 100 years. Gillingham and his team rode out the storm about 90 miles north of the plant, returning as soon as the wind subsided. Gillingham found his refinery under a foot or more of water, far less than he anticipated. Still, the damage was immense.

Normally, the refinery's generators run all the time, Gillingham said. But they had shut the machines down before the storm. Restarting them proved problematic.

Like other refineries, Valero gathered up workers and found a way to feed and house them on-site, first by Valero volunteers, then a professional catering service.

Valero opened a temporary gas station, supplying fuel to police, firefighters, ambulances and any other responders in need for the first 10 days. "Just come get it," they told them. The refinery didn't keep logs or charge for the critical fuel.

"We were going through 3 or 4,000 bags of ice a day. Of course, when you've got 1,700 people working in 100-degree, 100 percent humidity, they drink a lot of stuff," Gillingham told CNN.

Within three weeks, the refinery was up and running.

Motiva's Port Arthur plant also sits in close proximity to surrounding neighborhoods, employing around 900 people on its 3,600 acre home. The refinery converts close to 275,000 barrels of crude oil each day. First operated as Texas Company (Texaco) in 1903, two years after the Spindletop discovery, the refinery now is jointly owned by Shell and Saudi Refining. Their products include gasoline, jet fuel, diesel and heating oil, #6 oil and additional products. It is the largest single lube plant in the U.S.

During his 30 years with Motiva in Louisiana and Texas, Port Arthur Plant Manager Tom Purvis and his refinery have had more hurricane experience than they would like.

"We've had a lot of practice in refining our detailed emergency management plan. Once the winds get to a certain point, we decide to shut it down. The next decision is whether to evacuate. We will take everybody out of here and lock the gate, which is what we did during Rita."

Around 40 emergency responders, key operations and maintenance staff took the refinery's emergency equipment to Lumberton on Thursday to protect it from potential flooding.

"It was a real possibility with Rita that Port Arthur would be isolated. We easily could have been flooded. When Rita was approaching she was a category 5. We looked at that and thought, well, we hadn't seen a storm of that magnitude and we didn't know if we would be safe or not," Purvis said.

Evacuating was a prudent decision for someone who had watched a Pascagoula, Miss. refinery shut down for months because of flooding.

"We were in a safe, strong building, so I wasn't worried about that. My biggest concern was all the possible destruction to the refinery, and of course, to the lives of people who work here."

While some people went to sleep as Rita struck and didn't get up until the next morning, Purvis didn't. At 3 a.m. or so, the building lost power and alarms went off.

"I thought, damn, where did that come from?" Purvis said. "If you can sleep through that, you can sleep through anything. It was a pretty wild night."

The next morning, a small group of industry leaders and first re-sponders headed back. Purvis and his team of three had a hard time getting through because of downed power lines and debris. His electrical guy was able to check lines to see if they were live. Luckily, they didn't run into any.

In Port Arthur, flooded streets prevented them from getting to the plant, so they entered through the neighboring Huntsman plant.

The team was relieved to see the plant's process equipment and con-trol centers were in good shape and no leaks threatened the safety of the crew or its neighbors. The buildings, especially the 1940's-era main office building, were pretty badly damaged, though not destroyed.

The first priority was to provide for returning workers. The Port Arthur refinery got a lot of help from its corporate office in Houston, which already had requests in for temporary housing because of Hur-ricane Katrina's damage to the New Orleans refinery. They set up a small city in the refinery with 120 to 130 trailers and a covered serving tent where they provided meals around the clock to their workers and con-tract workers who were helping get functions restored.

The refinery also made arrangements to clear trees and provide por-table generators, blue roofs and plywood for employees' houses to help dry them out.

"Getting them squared away was a high priority. We also did much of the same for emergency responders for the cities in South and Mid-

County. We provided anything we could, including portable pumps and equipment anywhere it was needed. We also did a lot of outreach with various organizations to provide services."

Once they were able to get their generators hooked up and power somewhat restored, the refinery helped meet one of the area's most desperate needs when it provided fuel to police, fire departments and South and Mid-County city public buildings to help restore city functions. They also fueled the State Troopers and National Guard personnel.

Motiva has a long history of working with the community, Purvis said.

"They are our friends and neighbors and employees, and we feel an obligation. There was no debate. We were proactive and reactive when we were asked for help. Many folks helped who never will get the recognition they deserve because they were out there helping on their own. There was a lot of outreach we don't even know about and for which we will never be able to thank those folks."

Purvis was impressed that no one sat around waiting for someone else to help.

"There wasn't a lot of whining. They just went out and got it done."

He also has praise for community officials who were "out there doing what they need to do in a very proactive way, especially the police and firefighters who stepped up to the plate and did a great job under very difficult circumstances."

It took his refinery a month to get back up and running.

Chapter Four

Medical Evacuation

Once Carl Griffith's phone started ringing, it never stopped. In addition to making decisions and arrangements for the safety of the 252,000 people in his county, Griffith was fielding calls from judges in smaller, rural counties who had no experience with evacuations. Rita produced many firsts: one of them was the first time a mandatory evacuation was called for counties north of Jefferson County. Prior to Rita, their only substantial involvement had been with traffic control, law enforcement and lodging.

The call that disturbed Griffith the most was from Jack Colley, head of the Department of Public Safety Texas Division of Emergency Management. Griffith had put in requests to the state for ambulances and buses to help transport people out who didn't have the means to evacuate, including special needs people. Colley had to deliver the awful news that they simply weren't available because they already had been committed to Houston, Galveston and Corpus Christi where the storm was projected to hit before it changed course on Wednesday.

That left only one viable option – and it seemed a long shot.

"I knew the only way we were going to get all those people to safety was through a military airlift," Griffith said. "Clearly, it was a personal issue. I felt responsible for every person who lived in the county and to make sure we provided the best protection we possibly could. Knowing the size of the storm and vividly remembering the pictures of the devastation of Katrina, I had a lot of anxiety. I took it very, very seriously."

Griffith began receiving disturbing calls from hospitals and nursing homes telling him they had no way to get their people out. Most of the nursing homes had evacuation plans, as required by the regulatory agencies. Many were sketchy, at best. Even those with more detailed plans with contracts for buses and ambulances were helpless when the contracts couldn't be honored. No one had thought to have back-up plans for a situation like Katrina/Rita.

Those calls "ratcheted up" Griffith's anxiety. He began calling on the contacts he had built during his 18 years in public service. He put in a call to Texas Governor Rick Perry and several members of the Texas house and senate.

Griffith knew Perry was trying to help, he said, but the governor hadn't yet succeeded. Griffith was getting nowhere fast with others from the state, as well.

Meanwhile, a team that included Coast Guard Commander Capt. Sharon Richey, Port Arthur Fire Department Training Chief Wayne Roccaforte and Port Arthur Fire Chief Larry Richard had been placing their own calls to the White House Situation Room, telling them thousands of people were about to die if emergency responders didn't get them out.

"Are you going to help?" they asked.

"I was feeling helpless," Griffith said. "I knew that if we didn't get them airlifted out, people were going to die. Here we are in the greatest country in the world where we should be able to do anything, and it looked like politics was going to get in the way."

Finally, Griffith, a Democrat, called Kay Bailey Hutchison, the Republican Senior U.S. Senator from Texas.

"I had called other senators and the governor's office but was unable to secure any aircraft. I called Jamie Moore, Senator Hutchison's point person, and laid everything out, including my frustrations. He was very patient and listened to my concerns," Griffith said. "Within a couple of hours the White House Situation Room called me saying Senator Hutchison had called them and wanted to see this happen."

Hutchison "broke the log jam," Griffith said, and he credits her with helping save many lives. She credits her staff with making the right phone calls that secured clearance for the airlift.

Moore, Hutchison's Senior Policy Advisor, and Deputy Chief of Staff James Christoferson worked around the clock making sure they could respond to this crisis, Hutchison said. Her office's close contact with former Texas Governor and then President George W. Bush paid off.

As a member of the Defense Appropriations Committee, Hutchison worked closely with the Department of Defense, which called on to step in.

"We knew that DOD had the capacity – but they don't usually get involved in an emergency. It's usually done through FEMA. But this was such a huge hit on the heels of Katrina because so many communities were affected."

Having a political network in place makes all the difference, Hutchison said. It truly is who you know that counts.

"The county judges knew if they called us that we would have the contacts that would make things happen. Of course Carl was great to work with because he was on top of everything. He never gave up. Once he found out we could produce, we were in constant contact."

Hutchison didn't stop with helping Southeast Texas; she arranged for generators in Smith and other unaffected counties to be delivered to Angelina and Nacogdoches Counties, both of which had shelters that were without power because of storm damage. Stephen F. Austin University in Nacogdoches was filled to capacity with evacuees, she noted.

For Steve Curran, participating in the phone call that brought the good news was a distinct honor.

"The hard work the EMS group that was making phone calls to the White House Situation Room and all the hard work that Judge Griffith and Senator Hutchison had done, along with and Sen. John Cornyn, finally made the coordination of the airlift take place. I got to participate in that phone call. It was Judge Griffith, Metro Care EMS Paramedic Supervisor Kyle Knupple and myself."

On the other end of the conference call were the Department of Energy, along with the United States Marine Corps, Army, Navy and Air Force generals. The group discussed which planes would go to which locations.

Griffith and Curran had other calls to make. The hospitals, nursing homes, home health agencies and Jefferson County Health Department had been making frantic calls asking just how they were going to get their patients out. Now, the team had to direct them to the airport.

Despite a restless night, Southeast Texas Regional Airport Director Hal Ross had arrived an hour and a half hour before the evacuation order was to go out at 6 a.m. Thursday. He began implementing the airport's emergency plan. At the time, he said, it was little more than charging satellite phones, notifying the tower, the Transportation Security Administration and the airlines that the airport would be shut down, then securing property.

The small airport sits on 1,180 acres between Beaumont and Nederland. It has two runways equipped with Instrument Landing System (ILS) and approach markers for commercial and private aircraft, and an FAA-operated control tower. The main terminal has 45,000 square feet. In 2005, it had only one commercial airline, Continental, which offered flights to Houston.

Early Thursday, Continental Airlines management and airport operations manager Chris Clary decided that the 8:30 a.m. flight would be the last commercial one out. Ross closed the terminal and released his staff so they could make preparations to evacuate their families. He figured that by 11, he could be on the road to Lumberton High School, the designated emergency operations center. He would take a fuel or fire truck, four firemen and his maintenance foreman with him to ride out the storm.

Around 7:30 a.m. he noticed a missed call on his cell phone. It was Jefferson County Judge Carl Griffith.

"I'll always remember his words," Ross said. "I kept the message on my voice mail for four years until I got a new phone. He said, 'Hal, you're going to have to keep the airport open a while longer. We've got some planes coming in to pick up medical evacuees.'"

Planes? How many, he thought? What time would they arrive? And how many evacuees would they have to manage?

Ross started making calls for clarification but couldn't reach the key players in the emergency operations center. As judge of the largest county involved, Griffith was conferring with other judges and mayors about their needs. Every question brought to him needed an immediate answer – not next week, not tomorrow, not later that day. Now.

Port Arthur Police Deputy Chief John Owens and Port Neches Fire Department Chief and Emergency Management Coordinator Steve Curran, who were helping direct operations under Griffith's command at the EOC, also couldn't take his calls.

Ross notified tower personnel that they couldn't leave. Before any

Federal Aviation Agency airport can shut down, it must be cleared through the FAA in Washington.

Around 9 a.m. Ross got word to expect 80 medical special needs patients and that military aircraft would be coming in to carry out the evacuation, though he didn't know what kind of aircraft or what time. Ross relayed what little information he had to the tower and began clearing the terminal and secured it as the commercial airlines pulled out.

Then, he could do little but finish securing the airport, oversee the hangers, work with private plane owners to fly their aircraft out – and wait.

Around 9:30, an ambulance pulled in with the first patient.

"Here I am with this one lone fellow," Ross said. "We have no place to put him. The ambulance driver had one of those blue cushioned pads and they put the gentleman on it on the floor of the Jerry Ware Terminal, out of the way.

"Are you staying with the patient," Ross asked.

"No," the driver said, "We have other things to do." He drove off, leaving a stunned Ross with the semi-conscious patient.

Ross turned to one of the firefighters who had reported to the airport to help and asked, "How many EMTs do you have here?"

"There was only one fellow who looked like he was 22," Ross said, "So I told him, this is your patient and you're in charge. The rest of y'all, just do what you can."

"Not that I had any authority to direct the fire department or any other agency," Ross laughed, "which was a problem. The chain of command and organization was non-existent – but there was a lot of willingness, along with some reluctance, because nobody really knew what was going to happen."

A half hour later, Ross came back into the terminal to find five people in wheelchairs that had been dropped off. Then, he said, "Here comes this lady and her elderly mother in a small Toyota. Her father was a terminally ill cancer patient cared for at home. He was lying in the back seat on egg crate foam. I asked her, why are you coming here? She said, 'Well, it's on the radio that if you have special needs patients to bring them to the airport.'"

Ross had little choice. They unloaded the frail man and gently placed him next to the first patient on the floor of the terminal.

By then, others patients had been brought in on gurneys and stretchers, until 40 or so were clustered in the terminal.

Ross put in a couple of calls to Griffith and Owens at the county's emergency operations center but still couldn't get through. "They were up to their neck in other issues," he said.

Around 11:30 a.m. he got word that a C130 National Guard plane that had been helping with Hurricane Katrina was on its final approach. When it landed, Ross met the colonel in charge and introduced himself. "Before we get sidetracked, why are you here?" he asked. "We're here to assist you with the medical evacuation," the colonel replied.

"Do you have a medical staff?" Ross asked.

"That's what we are," the colonel said.

"OK," Ross said. "I run this airport and it's our job to take care of runways and all things associated with landing. These people over here," he said, pointing to the patients scattered across the floor, "that's your job and we will support you in any way we can as long as you tell me you are going to take care of all these people."

"Yes, Sir," the colonel said. "That's what we're here for."

Man, Ross thought to himself, this is wonderful.

The colonel, who had 30 or so Guardsmen on the fully equipped plane, looked around and asked Ross, "Do you have a larger place? From what I hear this isn't going to be big enough."

Not big enough? Ross thought. Exactly how many patients were expected – and what else didn't he know?

Ross sent airport maintenance manager Danny Nichols to take the colonel to the 45,000 sq foot main terminal that had been shut down.

"This is what we need," the colonel said.

Ross opened the main terminal and began doing the best he could to assuage the heat. In an unlucky piece of bad timing – Rita's hallmark – the main air conditioning unit had gone out the month before. Ross hooked up and started the small portable air conditioner that was all the terminal had.

The troops began moving patients the quarter mile from the Jerry Ware terminal to the main terminal. Desperate, they used any means of transportation they could find, including loading patients onto large luggage racks and wheeling them across the concrete.

At the height of the evacuation, buses loaded with patients were stacked up all the way from Highway 69 to the terminal. They were parked three abreast beneath the unloading canopy at the terminal, which created some stress for Ross.

"They were stacked end to end on the main entrance road, which would have prevented emergency personnel from getting to the terminal if there had been a fire or other emergency. It took about 15 hours to clear the line, from 7 p.m. Thursday night to 11 a.m. Friday," Ross said.

Across town at Christus St. Elizabeth Hospital, Administrator Mary Egan was being tested as she prepared to implement the hospital's emergency management plan. She had been administrator for the 400+ bed hospital – the largest in Southeast Texas – for barely a year, but, as she put it, "The buck stops here. I am the one who is ultimately responsible."

When Katrina evacuees began coming through Beaumont and stopped at Ford Park, doctors and nurses were on hand to tend to their health concerns, including staff from St. Elizabeth, as well as Beaumont's other hospital, Memorial Hermann Baptist Beaumont. The hospitals accepted patients with special medical needs, including pregnant women about to deliver.

Although St. Elizabeth reviews and updates its emergency plans after each disaster, caring for the evacuees of Hurricane Katrina for those three weeks provided hands-on lessons. As difficult as the experience was, it was a cake walk compared to safely evacuating critical needs patients in advance of Hurricane Rita.

St. Elizabeth's plan called for the smaller St. Mary Hospital in Port Arthur to evacuate first. At 7 feet above sea level, Port Arthur is one of the more vulnerable areas in Jefferson County. Only neighboring Sabine Pass, a small community of around 2,000 on the coast, is more vulnerable.

At some point, Egan knew, transportation would no longer be available, so she spent the first part of the week taking care of those most at risk. FEMA required all ambulances, EMS vehicles and other medical transportation vehicles to report in to be available for use.

Egan called in her contracts, scrambling to find ways to get the patients moved. She used aircraft, helicopters and ground transportation to move them to sister hospitals in Louisiana and to the larger Beaumont hospital according to the hospital's emergency plan.

Wednesday, FEMA issued a moratorium on emergency vehicles.

"They told us they would decide where all the emergency vehicles would go – and we would hear from them. That stopped our evacuation," she said.

Egan put in a frantic call to Judge Griffith, telling him she had 200 patients at St. Elizabeth needing to be transported out. Without ambulances, she told the judge, she couldn't move them.

Egan also was concerned about patients spending any more time than necessary at the airport. She had begun getting reports that conditions at the airport were grim. The lack of air-conditioning had sent patients' body temperatures soaring, increasing dehydration.

"I am a wild Irish woman and when I heard this, as you can image, I went ballistic," Egan said. "I called Carl and said, we've got to change this. I am not sending any of my critical care patients to the airport until I know your planes have landed. Then, you send the ambulances."

Several hours later, Egan got a call from an Air Force major who earlier had promised her that planes would be coming and they would be equipped with medical personnel.

The major said, "Mary, I've got some good news and some bad news."

"What's the good news? "

"The ambulances are here."

Hallelujah, Egan thought. What's the bad news?

"I don't have any medical personnel to attend to them."

Egan began asking her staff for volunteers who would be willing to go provide care. More than a dozen nurses said they would stay with the patients from beginning to end.

"The surgical patients needed pain medication and that requires a doctor," Egan said. "Some had brought their medications with them. Dr. Arsenio Martin and his wife, also a doctor, stayed there and helped administer medications to diabetics and other special needs patients."

After ambulances finally arrived at the hospital, personnel transported 72 of Mary Egan's remaining patients to the airport for evacuation. She had categorized patients according to condition. Some were able to be transported to the airport on buses, but Egan didn't want them to go unattended.

"I was a little uncomfortable with that. You can't just put a patient who has been hospitalized on a bus with only a bus driver. I was concerned for their safety. I was absolutely outraged at the fact there were buses that dropped patients off at the airport and just left them there. I felt whoever discharged those patients from the nursing homes or the hospital had the responsibility to keep those patients safe."

By late Thursday, Egan realized she couldn't get any more patients out.

"The problem is I still had 128 patients left here after the ambulatory and critical needs left on the planes. We had neo-natal intensive care unit babies and St. Mary's patients, too."

Among the 128 patients remaining under Egan's care was Sarah Garber, a 17-year-old Louisiana girl who sustained a catastrophic head injury in a car accident with her family while evacuating from Hurricane Katrina. On Thursday, when it became clear Sarah was not going to make it, the family talked to the doctors and nurses about Sarah's wishes to become an organ donor. Sarah's critical care nurse, Lynnae Mathews, knew that the Southwest Transplant Alliance team already had evacuated.

Mathews was determined to find a way to make sure Sarah's life went on by saving others. She called SWTA in Dallas and made a first-ever request. Could they come get Sarah? The team agreed to fly her to the Baylor Medical Center in Dallas.

Problem after problem threatened to make that impossible. FEMA had commandeered most air ambulances and finding a plane or helicopter would be difficult. Because Sarah's fatal injuries were caused by an auto accident and criminal charges likely would be filed against the other car's driver, a judge would have to authorize her release. The hospital also had to repeat tests to follow the hospital's procedures to confirm Sarah was brain dead.

The team refused to give up. SWTA somehow found a Southwest Airline pilot who said he had a plane in Oklahoma and would be happy to pick it up and fly in with a team.

The hospital arranged for an ambulance to be waiting at the airport.

"They were able to fly Sarah out in time to go to Baylor to donate the organs. There were four or five people who benefited from her donation," Egan said.

By the time Sarah's airlift left, Mathews had decided it was too late for her to evacuate and that she would stay and help move patients and secure the hospital. It also would allow her to care for Sarah's mother. As a mother of two daughters, Mathews felt a special kinship with her. She had promised to watch over Sarah as if she were her own child.

"One of the things I stress is that my nurses are empowered to do what's right for the patient," Egan said. "We just make it happen."

Meanwhile, evacuation efforts at the airport had escalated. While shutting down commercial air service that morning had opened up the terminal, making it available as a makeshift holding area, it also meant that the four cancelled flights left close to 100 people stranded when they showed up to catch their flights. Among the passengers were a doctor and his wife trying to get home. The doctor, looking around the terminal at all the patients, asked Ross what was going on. He explained that a medical evacuation was under way.

"Where are they going," the doctor asked.

"I don't have any idea," Ross said.

"If I stay here and help, will they fly me wherever they are going?'

Ross checked with the colonel in charge of the aircraft.

"Sure," he said.

Patients kept coming in all afternoon. When night fell, Ross walked through the terminal and counted more than 600 patients strapped to litters. In the center of the terminal sat around 70 patients in wheelchairs. There was a shortage of food and drinking water and the bathroom facilities had succumbed to the overwhelming numbers of people using them. Around 3 p.m. Thursday, the City of Nederland had shut down the water system, which created yet another problem because there was no water to the toilets.

There was very little air conditioning and the smell of waste and medical bio-hazards created a scene for Ross reminiscent of a triage unit in a military operation. Although he had a camera with him, Ross didn't feel comfortable taking photos of such misery. He's glad others had the foresight to document the scene for history.

The medical airlift brought together teams that otherwise wouldn't have connected, including the U.S. Coast Guard.

As Commanding Officer for Marine Safety at the U.S. Coast Guard station in Port Arthur, Sharon Richey directed all Coast Guard missions in the Beaumont/Port Arthur Unit, which covers High Island, Texas east to Lake Charles, La.

While deployed to Baton Rouge after Katrina, she got a taste of hurricane response, but never had been involved in preparation, other than attending one training exercise. Her previous stations in St. Louis and California didn't cover hurricanes and she wasn't involved in hurricane training during her two years in New Orleans.

A few days after Katrina the district office in New Orleans ordered Richey to report to Beaumont as the U.S. Coast Guard liaison to Secretary Michael Brown, director of FEMA. She was the point of contact with the state offices of emergency services and served as liaison to Bill Lokey, Federal Coordinating Officer, FEMA Response and Recovery for Katrina. Once Admiral Thad Allen became principal federal officer and brought in his crew, she helped in relocating to New Orleans.

Rita wasn't even on her radar screen, she recalled, but when Jefferson County began participating in conference calls to prepare for Rita, she joined in.

"At that point, the county didn't have a dedicated emergency management center. I had a brand new Marine Safety Unit in the Texas State Bank Building, and we had a fairly large space to conduct teleconferences from, so I offered it to the judge if he wanted it. He jumped on that."

While emergency operations center personnel were planning how to evacuate citizens, Richey had to focus on her staff. She evacuated all of her unit except for a group she dedicated to stay and help with citizen evacuation.

Richey's commitment to helping the people of Southeast Texas created conflict when her commanding officers ordered her to take the rest of the unit and evacuate. Because of their Katrina experience, her unit planned to evacuate early on to get them out of harm's way. Richey didn't feel right about that.

When the Coast Guard sent a C130 for her to use in evacuating the unit, Richey parked it at the Southeast Texas Regional Airport while she figured out how she could help with the massive evacuation of medical special needs folks about to take place.

"I told my crew that we weren't going to depart right then and to stand by. I basically was ordered out of the area, but I didn't want to go. What I did was I bought us a little time. I was in a dilemma. Do I disobey this order and suffer the consequences – or do I stay here? I really wanted to stay and go to Lumberton with the first responders."

When Griffith had realized that an airlift was the only answer for the medical special needs folks and started calling Senators Cornyn and Hutchison, Richey briefed her command that they needed to help if they could.

"I'm not sure how it all happened, but military aircraft started coming into the airport and that's how we ended up transporting the people who had no other way out."

When the first responders ran out of drivers, members of Richey's unit helped drive buses carrying nursing home patients and special needs people without transportation. Once the military planes started coming in, Richey noticed that everyone there was doing their best to load the more than 8,000 passengers but they were extremely short-handed.

"The Transportation Security Administration guy basically was coordinating that airlift. Some people in disasters dig in and help. Other people don't. There were a lot of people there who rolled up their sleeves and said we've got to help, even though it may or may not have been their job. I took whatever people I had and sprinkled them throughout the airport to help with the process. If you can imagine nursing home patients on stretchers in an airport ... It was so hot. So hot. It was a flurry of activity."

Richey told the crew of her C130 that they were going to have to stay until she felt comfortable that they had helped local emergency responders get as many people out as possible. She put her air crew to work as well.

"These are guys who are used to flying airplanes – and they are loading people onto military aircraft."

Richey held the crew as long as she possibly could. When the local fire chiefs and first responders told her they were at the point where they felt everyone would make it out and she no longer felt that she was "leaving people high and dry," Richey and her unit boarded their aircraft and left sometime after midnight, in the early hours of Friday morning.

Richey overruled one last directive. Instead of flying to Corpus Christi as planned, she directed the flight crew to make a quick run to Lake Charles to pick up several of her junior officers. The winds already were high, but the crew landed, got the rest of her unit on board, including one officer's dog, and took off.

When it comes to leadership, Richey said she saw it demonstrated time and again during the Rita evacuation from people like Brit Featherston and Carl Griffith.

"To me, the judge was one of those elected officials who rolled up his sleeves and said, 'Guys we've got to make this happen and we have to do it right.' He made things happen and everybody rallied around him. I was impressed with that. Plus I was impressed by Chief Curran and all the other fire chiefs."

Everyone available to help kept busy unloading patients from several 50-passenger buses that brought them to the airport for evacuation and by 11 that night, the first three military aircraft left full of special needs people.

Crews continued to work through the night as patients kept arriving. By 4 o'clock Friday morning, the patient count had swollen to several thousand. While Ross was checking out progress on one of the buses, he was surprised to see the volunteer doctor still checking patients.

"Sir, you've been at this a long time. Don't you want to take a break?"

The doctor lifted his head, looked at Ross and said, "I still have patients to tend to."

In the midst of all the activity and confusion, Ross never caught the Good Samaritan's name. All he knows is he was from somewhere in the Northeast. Ross has wished a hundred times he could tell him how much his care for all those people he didn't even know meant to them, their families and those entrusted with their care.

By 3 p.m. Friday, Ross finally could see the 30-plus-hour ordeal coming to a close. Two C-17 planes took off back to back, marking the last flights out.

Later, Ross would learn that the medical and special needs evacuation had produced another record. It was the largest military airlift of its kind in U.S. history. Incredibly, those who had joined together to unload patients, tend to them, then hand carry them onto the planes under the most adverse conditions imaginable had managed to send more than 8,000 people to safety.

"I don't know exactly how everything transpired in securing the planes, but because of them, we were able to airlift 8,300 people out of harm's way," Ross said.

All in all, an estimated 40 military aircraft were involved, including C-5, C-9, C-17, 737 and C-130 planes. They flew patients to facilities that had agreed to take them in 16 different states.

The process had been significantly slowed by the requirement from the Transportation Security Administration for screening of all patients before they could board any evacuation aircrafts. Because this was the first military airlift Jefferson County had utilized for a hurricane evacuation of medical special needs folks – a last-ditch resort – confusion reigned. Patients didn't have medical records with them and didn't have designated destinations.

Even with hastily drawn manifests, it would take days for all the patients to be located. Officials couldn't tell families where their loved ones were going because they didn't know. Even after patients were located, the Health Insurance Portability and Accountability Act (HIPPA) of 1996 protecting patients' privacy kept the authorities from telling them, adding more stress and anguish to Rita's victims.

After the storm, when people sat around talking about all the things that happened, misinformation about the airlift began circulating. Perhaps the one that generated the most arguments was about buses loaded with patients being driven directly onto the planes because there wasn't enough time to unload them all. While the massive belly of the largest planes could have handled that, it simply didn't happen.

What is true is that a representative with the U.S. Transportation Command (TRANSCOM) from Scott Air Force Base, Ill., which was overseeing the airlift, called Griffith and asked for permission to do just that. Griffith gave his consent. But it ended up not being necessary, Ross said, and to the best of his and his staff's knowledge, each person was carefully hand-carried onto the planes.

Below: Hurricane Rita's path. *NOAA image*

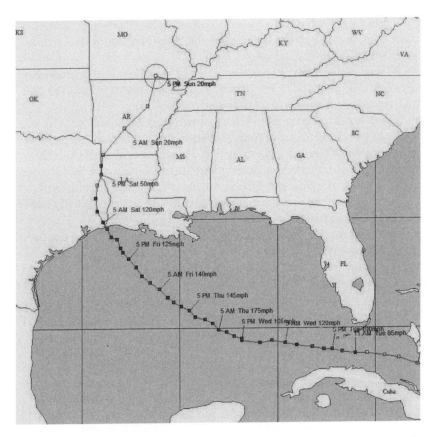

ABOVE: Traffic backed up for miles and came to a complete stop for long periods as citizens fled prior to Rita's landfall, like this parking lot on Interstate 45 in Houston.

BELOW: A patient is carried aboard a C-141 Starlifter during the medical evacuation prior to Rita. Airmen from the 433rd Aeromedical Evacuation Squadron at Lackland Air Force Base, Texas, and the 183rd AES from the Mississippi Air National Guard conducted the evacuation along with Air Force, Coast Guard and Navy aircraft. *U.S. Air Force Photo by Master Sgt. Lance Cheung*

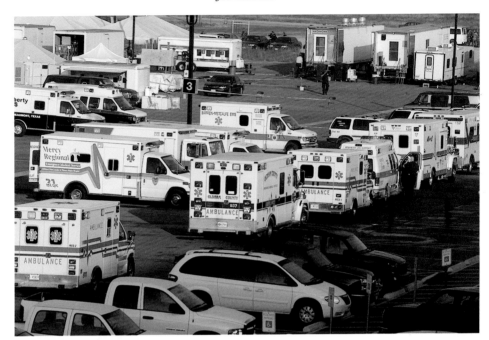

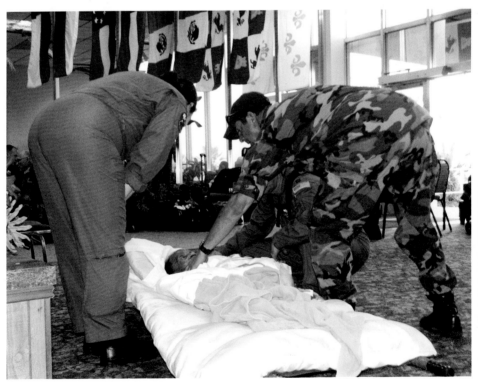

ABOVE: The U.S. Post Office in the community of Sabine Pass lies in ruin after Hurricane Rita blew ashore near the small fishing village. *Photo: Jennifer Reynolds/Beaumont Enterprise*

OPPOSITE TOP: Hundreds of ambulances called into action to help evacuate medical special needs people await use. *Photo: Beaumont Fire Department*

OPPOSITE BOTTOM: Members of the military prepare patients for an air evacuation in the old terminal building at the Southeast Texas Regional Airport as Hurricane Rita bears down on the coast. *Photo: Roger Cowles/Port Arthur News*

BELOW: Hurricane Rita's storm surge pushed boats inland at Sabine Pass. *Photo: Steve Buser*

ABOVE: Photographer Bart Bragg, owner of Cricchio-Bragg Photography, surveys the destruction at his studio. *Photo: Roger Cowles/Port Arthur News*

LEFT: The Port Arthur Dairy Queen was badly damaged by Hurricane Rita's fierce winds.
Photo: Jerry Jordan/The Examiner

BELOW: Downed trees and power lines made roads treacherous. *Photo: Beaumont Fire Department*

ABOVE: Member of the Beaumont Fire Department work to control a fire at the Elks Lodge that erupted when electricity was restored. *Photo: Beaumont Fire Department*

BELOW: A convenience store in Port Arthur lies in pieces after Rita's hurricane force winds. *Photo: Jerry Jordan/Examiner*

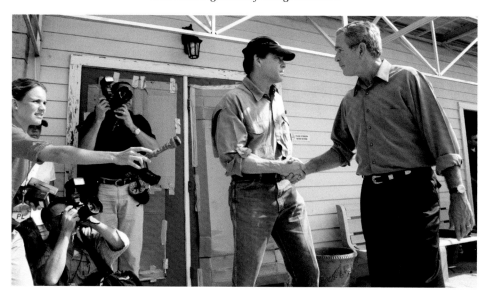

ABOVE: Port Arthur, TX, Sept. 27, 2005- President George W. Bush and Texas governor Rick Perry hold a brief question and answer session at the Southeast Texas Regional Airport. *Photo by Ed Edahl/FEMA*

OPPOSITE TOP: Rita's winds downed millions of trees across Southeast and East Texas, damaging and destroying homes in the process. *Photo: Beaumont Fire Department*

OPPOSITE BOTTOM: Humane Society groups rescued loose dogs after Rita, providing food, water and shelter. *Photo: Texas Forest Service*

BELOW: A hand-lettered sign alerts passers-by that desperately-needed food, water and ice are available. *Photo: Beaumont Fire Department*

ABOVE: A lone bulb was the only source of light at the EOC at Edison Plaza after Rita destroyed the electrical grid system. *Photo: Beaumont Fire Department*

BELOW: Citizens who stayed behind were desperate for food, water, ice and other daily needs. WalMart was one of the first stores to reopen when power was restored.
Photo: Beaumont Fire Department

ABOVE: Senator Kay Bailey Hutchison, center, gives a press briefing at Ford Park. Also pictured, from left, FEMA's Gary Jones and David Paulison, Port Arthur Mayor Oscar Ortiz, U.S. Coast Guard Admiral Larry Hereth and Steve McCraw (Texas Dept. of Homeland Security).
Photo: Beaumont Fire Department

BELOW: Beaumont Firefighter Charlie Cox eagerly reads the special edition of the Beaumont Enterprise, the first paper it was able to print after Rita. *Photo: Beaumont Fire Department*

ABOVE: Four days after the storm, first responders work from the emergency operations center to restore their cities, including Chester Jourdan, seated, in red Lamar University cap; Beaumont Fire Capt. Pat Grimes, seated, in yellow shirt; and Beaumont Fire Capt. Brad Parsons, seated.

Photo: Beaumont Fire Department

RIGHT: Beaumont Police Department Public Information Officers Carmen Apple and Cindy Ball check the latest information on Rita Recovery.

Photo: Beaumont Fire Department

ABOVE: Exhausted utility workers take time to grab a night meal after working 12 hours to restore power. *Photo: Entergy Texas, Inc.*

BELOW: Utility crews came from across the country to assist Entergy in restoring power, sleeping in tent cities during the first few days after Hurricane Rita. *Photo: Entergy Texas, Inc.*

ABOVE: U.S. Senator John Cornyn speaks during a visit to the Jefferson County EOC at the Elegante Hotel in Beaumont. *Photo: Beaumont Fire Department*

BELOW: The heavily damaged Port Arthur Police Department offers a sign to let citizens know they are open and on the job. *Photo: Jerry Jordan/Examiner*

ABOVE: Judge Carl Griffith conducts a briefing at the Elegante in Beaumont. From left, Nederland Mayor Dick Nugent, Port Neches Mayor Glenn Johnson, Beaumont Mayor Guy Goodson and Jefferson County Commissioner Mark Domingue. *Photo: Beaumont Fire Department*

RIGHT: President George W. Bush asked to speak with Jefferson County Judge Carl Griffith in private before holding a press conference at the Southeast Texas Regional Airport. *Photo: Hal Ross*

ABOVE: The Vidor Church of Christ in Vidor, TX lost its roof after Hurricane Rita blew in its stained glass window. *Bob McMillan/FEMA Photo*

BELOW: Emergency response crews posted points of distribution where citizens could get food, ice and water. *Photo: Texas Forest Service*

ABOVE: Jefferson County Health Director Dr. Cecil Walkes, left, helped guide medical response after the hurricane. *Photo: Beaumont Fire Department*

LEFT: A DMAT team from Massachusetts came to the aid of the medical staff at Memorial Hermann Baptist Hospital. *Photo: FEMA*

RIGHT: Principal Christi Heid, fourth from left, accepts a check for Sabine Pass school collected by the students of the Sam D. Bundy School in Farmville, NC. *Photo FEMA*

ABOVE: Southern Baptist Men help load supplies for the Salvation Army during Hurricane Rita recovery. *Photo: Beaumont Fire Department*

BELOW: Brit Featherston, in the blue striped shirt, and Matt Orwig, gray suit, pose for a photo with members of the Buddhist Compassion Relief Group, Tzu Chi. *Photo: Beaumont Fire Department*

Chapter Five

Gridlock

Days before Rita roared inland, she already was deal-
ing out misery. The nightmare evacuation of medical and other special
needs citizens by the military was completed mere hours before increasing winds made flying impossible.

Simultaneously, officials faced another major obstacle – the evacuation of the general population with the issuance of a mandatory evacuation beginning at 6 a.m. Thursday.

The Katrina effect already had people on edge. Could what happened
in New Orleans happen here, they wondered? What would we do? Getting out of town seemed like a no-brainer and many hundreds of thousands of people were making that difficult decision at the same time.

Rita complicated matters with her wavering course. For a successful
evacuation, officials have to give citizens enough time to safely leave the
area. But if they call for the evacuation too soon, the storm can change
course, creating multiple problems from loss of income to extra vehicles
on the road when people who don't need to leave, do.

That was the case with Rita.

Emergency evacuations are done in stages; those closest to the coast
are the first to leave. Next come the low-lying cities and communities

just inland. Officials know that many citizens will ignore the call to let the areas most at risk evacuate first, thinking only of their needs. What officials didn't expect was other cities interfering with the instructions.

Rita's unpredictable path, along with the Katrina fear factor, forced Houston Mayor Bill White and Harris County Judge Robert Eckels to make a decision about how they would handle evacuation. On Wednesday, Rita was predicted to come in near Galveston, which would put the island and parts of the Houston area at risk. While the storm was still a little under three days out, White and Eckels made the call for a mandatory evacuation that included areas that were not in harm's way, even if the storm had hit Houston dead on.

At a live press conference at 9:30 a.m. Wednesday, Sept. 21, White and Eckels announced that they were requesting voluntary evacuation of "those living in flood-prone areas, storm surge areas and mobile homes. Mandatory evacuations will begin for persons living in Zone A at 6 p.m. today, 2 a.m. Thursday for those in Zone B, and 6 a.m. Thursday for those in Zone C. Mandatory evacuation also will be in place for Houstonians living within the storm surge area, living in areas that typically flood, and for anyone who lives in a mobile home."

That announcement by a visibly shaken White and Eckels effectively sealed off escape routes for anyone to the south of the city.

By the time the storm veered toward Sabine Pass, the roads that the coastal communities east of Houston needed for evacuation already were packed.

According to an Association of Schools of Public Health Report in 2006, Harris County emergency evacuation models had predicted 800,000 to 1.2 million people would evacuate. More than twice that took to the roads, making it the largest evacuation in the history of the United States. Somewhere between 2.5 and 3 million people left Southeast Texas, the majority of them from the Galveston/Houston area.

Houston, the nation's fourth most populous city, has a million and a quarter citizens. Added to that was Jefferson County at 247,322 and Orange County at 84,245 – and that's not counting the many thousands of Hurricane Katrina evacuees still in Southeast Texas.

The primary evacuation route for those in Jefferson County is Highway 69/96/287 north. Smaller roads feed into the highway that most people took. Unfortunately, Houston area traffic not only paralyzed Interstate 45 north, but 69/96/287 as well.

"What happened in the Houston Metro area literally paralyzed traffic just north of Beaumont. You got up to the Lumberton area, and it was bumper to bumper all the way up to Longview. I've heard stories that it went all the way to Texarkana, where our designated shelter was," John Owens said.

"That is directly attributed to a metro area of around 3 million people panicking and leaving. With the exception of Trinity Bay and Galveston Bay south of Interstate 10, there was no reason to leave Houston," Owens said. "I'm from Houston, and my mother lives off 290 in Northwest Houston. The distance from her house to Trinity Bay is about 130 miles – and she is evacuating? I said, 'Mom, you don't need to evacuate.' She said, 'The Judge of Harris County said we have to evacuate.'

"When a county judge gets on television and tells you 'Get out, get out!' – and you figure in the Katrina effect, you're leaving," Owens said. "So you had that huge metropolitan area paralyzing not only the interstate, but all the arteries east of 35 all the way up into Dallas and points east of there to Texarkana."

During the thickest part of the evacuation, traffic was at a virtual standstill for 100 miles. When traffic did move, it was measured in inches. Tail lights blinked on and off, on and off, for hours. It took as long as three hours to move five miles. When possible, drivers turned the engines off to conserve fuel. Gas stations along the route began to run out of gas. Long lines waited at those that did still have fuel, hoping to get gas before they ran out. To complicate matters further, even stations that had gas and could pump it didn't have the means to accept credit cards because communication lines were cut off.

Hurricane Rita couldn't have chosen a worse time to hit. Air temperatures stayed at or over 100 degrees and humidity hovered at 94 percent. As the air temperature rose, so did the body temperature of elderly and ill evacuees trapped inside autos for up to 24 hours. The constant stop and go forced drivers to shut off the air conditioning to avoid overheating and to conserve fuel. Even that couldn't save many. The highway shoulders were dotted with cars that failed. People waiting in line helped push them out of the way.

Those who hadn't brought food and water emptied shelves of the grocery and convenience stores still open along the way. At least one pet went into convulsions while the owner poured water over its body to try to bring the temperature down. With highways turned into parking lots, emergency medical workers had a hard time responding in a timely manner to evacuees' medical emergencies.

Kind souls who lived along the evacuation route passed out cups of cold water. Bathroom facilities were scarce, and those who were able to move only a few miles in three hours resorted to relieving themselves in place, using towels and spare clothing to try to protect what little modesty they had left.

The Texas Department of Transportation sent courtesy patrols with gas and water to pass out along the route, but it was limited. Texas Homeland Security Director Steve McCraw told the Cox News Service that even though officials tried to position 100 refueling vehicles on the road, they were stuck in traffic like everyone else.

Although the death toll from Rita was low, thanks in no small part to the medical special needs airlift, there was no method in place to track those whose deaths were a by-product of the evacuation. Many elderly and ill folks died within months after the ordeal. Stress and increased body temperatures for an extended period of time indisputably were factors.

Some lucky folks took back roads and looped around, but even then it didn't save them much time. State troopers and local law enforcement had blocked access to the larger roads. Frustrated and worried folks found they had no option but to sit in unbearable heat.

State officials hadn't anticipated the number of cars that would take to the road, so initially, contraflow lanes weren't designated. Contraflow, which turns southbound lanes on the freeway into northbound, is a risky proposition. The sheer number of roads that feed into the freeway system make it almost impossible for law enforcement officials to monitor and turn back southbound vehicles, increasing the chance for accidents.

As traffic came to a standstill on Thursday, Gov. Rick Perry ordered Interstate 10 and Interstate 45 opened for contraflow. By late Thursday, TXDOT tried to follow suit with contraflow on US. 69 from its split from U.S. 96 north, but ran into major problems with logistics. Drivers who saw 69 had contraflow assumed the same would be true of 96. It was not. TXDOT called the contraflow effort to a halt.

During evacuations, the Governor's Office of Emergency Management's State Operations Center (SOC) makes the decision and implements the plan in coordination with officials in the coastal communities and further inland along the designated evacuation route. The Disaster District Committee(s) (DDCs) and Regional Liaison Officers (RLOs) usually are the intermediaries passing along information.

Once evacuation starts, traffic management responsibilities are assigned to applicable law enforcement agencies by a Department of Public Safety Plan, according to Owens. DPS still had overall responsibility, but local police had assignments as well. Port Arthur police had to staff intersections along Highway 87 (Gulfway Drive) and Highway 69 to make sure intersecting streets along the evacuation route were barricaded.

Once evacuees moved a little further inland from the storm, stopping at the closest motel was not an option, even for those who could afford it. Rooms weren't merely in short supply; there simply weren't any because hotels as far north as Arkansas were completely booked.

Those who couldn't afford a motel room or whose cars had overheated or run out of gas stopped at the shelter hubs pre-determined for evacuees. Beaumont residents were directed to a shelter in Tyler, while Port Arthur residents were sheltered in Texarkana.

After the devastating hurricane season in Florida in 2004, Gov. Rick Perry called for the state's Office of Homeland Security to assess Texas' evacuation plans. The OHS gave its recommendations in March 2005.

Beaumont hosted the Third Annual Texas Hurricane Conference in May 2005, where the Governor's Division of Emergency Management provided workshops based on the revised evacuation plans. During the conference, the state introduced two new concepts: Shelter Hubs and Evacuation Information Centers.

Shelter hubs are "pre-identified geographical locations enabling state officials along with local partners to rapidly open core shelters, deploy mass care resources, and gather information for critical decision-making," according to a 2006 Association of Schools of Public Health report.

The hubs "include public facilities large enough to serve as shelters and facilities to warehouse supplies and personnel" while Evacuation Information Centers are "roadside facilities located at highway rest stops that are designed to assist evacuees leaving or returning to a community. They are supposed to provide information to the public and to shelter staff deploying resources to the affected area. These centers have been planned to provide restroom facilities, immediate emergency assistance, and fuel, but not food and shelter."

The State of Texas Emergency Management Plan controls evacuations and gives elected officials the authority to "order evacuations; prescribe routes, modes, and destinations; and control disaster area ingress and egress" in the 22 Texas counties that are vulnerable to hurricane storm surge and winds.

The state designates shelter hubs once the involved cities agree to provide the facilities. It's a huge undertaking and many of the cities were unprepared for the sheer number of folks evacuating. Some residents arrived at a shelter only to find it at capacity.

Because the storm maintained enough strength to disrupt electrical grids as far inland as Lufkin, thousands of evacuees had to leave their shelters and find another one.

One of the areas that agreed to be designated as a shelter hub was Lufkin/Nacogdoches. The City of Lufkin was prepared to shelter 10,000 evacuees. The shelter opened Wednesday afternoon and was completely filled by Thursday night. By Friday the official shelter population hit 17,000 in the 35 official shelters in Angelina County. The American Red Cross shelters picked up thousands more.

In the City of Lufkin's Hurricane Rita Aftermath Review in February 2006, it reported that by Friday Sept. 23, the city "became completely overwhelmed with traffic and the demand for supplies."

The scene was repeated in other shelter hubs, where cities would learn how much more was expected from their commitment than they knew when they first agreed. But as chaotic as citizens found the evacuation and conditions in the shelter cities, they were much better off than those who stayed behind.

Chapter Six

Media

During a mandatory evacuation, it falls to manage-
ment of smaller businesses to make decisions on how they will handle
the storm and what they will require of employees. Most encourage
everyone to leave.

For the media, it's a tough call. Their job is keeping the public informed – and that means being there for the big events. The competitive
drive is strong, even when a major hurricane is edging closer by the hour.

At KFDM, management pushed for a complete evacuation, effectively
shutting the station down. Bostwick and several other staffers volunteered to stay to keep reporting on the storm.

"A group of five of us – me, reporter Sally McDonald, producer Scott
Lawrence, Dan Gresham and Bill Leger – lobbied very strongly that we
would stay. We pled with the station manager to let us keep the station
on as long as we could. Not to be heroes, but to pass along information
that the world needed to hear," Bostwick said.

Station Manager Larry Beaulieu agreed to let the crew stay.

Members of the media knew their job was to keep the public informed. What they didn't know was how desperate everyone would
become for the tiniest bit of news – and that they would provide that

lifeline.

As he watched Hurricane Rita enter the Gulf of Mexico, Jerry Jordan had a bad feeling. After working the coastline of Mississippi and Alabama during Hurricane Katrina as the news editor for Beaumont's weekly Examiner newspaper, he had learned what a storm of that magnitude can do. He'd snapped photos of the marks on doorways that showed where bodies had been removed. He'd seen mile after mile of homes pushed back and tossed into piles like kindling.

Jordan had awakened his wife about a week before Hurricane Rita and said, "We're going to get hit by this hurricane."

"Jerry," she said, "you always look for the negative."

"No," he told her, "I've just got a feeling about this storm."

The discussion escalated into a fight. At the time, the couple lived more than 40 miles from Beaumont in Kirbyville and Jordan's wife worked at a paper mill in Louisiana. He told her, "You need to listen to me; this is going to be bad."

"You just want it to come here," she told her husband.

"No," he told her. "I want it to go anywhere but here, but yeah, it's going to hit here and when it does, it's going to be news."

Like other news media, the weekly's management left it up to the employees whether they would evacuate or stay and work.

"We don't make people stay. It's a voluntary thing," Jordan said. "If you want to stay, great. I appreciate it. But if you stay, you're going to work because then I'm taking responsibility for you."

Jordan and Copy Editor Joshua Cobb decided to stay. They rode out the storm at the paper's downtown Beaumont offices, which once had been a bank and had a large, walk-in safe.

During Katrina, while chasing the storm across Louisiana, Mississippi and Alabama, Jordan learned how inadequately prepared he was for a hurricane. Between Katrina and Rita, he assembled a "Go kit" filled with energy drinks, energy bars, an emergency medical kit, ropes, a tire-repair kit and anything else he can fit inside a 2x3 Rubbermaid plastic bin. He also carries a chain saw and extra gas cans.

"My biggest fear was running out of gas. I learned that lesson in Katrina. There was no fuel. I had to drive from Biloxi back to Baton Rouge to get fuel. You are working all day and it's nighttime when you get done. So I'm on the road at midnight driving to Baton Rouge to fill up and then I have to use part of that fuel to get back to Gulfport."

Jordan loves to chase the big stories, and the more danger involved, the better he likes it. But he has his limits.

Before Rita, Jordan was at Walter Umphrey State Park taking photos when a weather-beaten satellite van rolled up. Out stepped Geraldo Rivera. When Jordan introduced himself, Rivera told him he was trying to get to Holly Beach, La.

"Can you help us?"

"Yeah, I'll be glad to help anyway I can or take you anywhere you want to go, but I'm not taking you to Holly Beach," Jordan told him. "Once you go over that bridge, it's flat. If this storm comes in, Holly Beach is going to be underwater. I promise you, if you go there, you will die. That's a suicide mission."

Instead, Jordan took them to Sabine Pass, where he explained several times that the community name was pronounced Suh-Bean Pass. Unfailingly, every time Rivera reported, he called it Sab-Bean, annoying the locals to no end, Jordan said, laughing.

After leading Rivera in, Jordan hung around Sabine Pass for a while, until the wind gusts grew to around 75 mph.

"I got nervous, but not because I was in the wind," he said. "I knew the one thing I could not control was something hitting the truck and causing a mechanical failure. And my cell phone was dead. I had a bad feeling, so I turned around and came back to Port Arthur."

Much of the "outside" media had congregated at the walking pier by the ship channel at the park behind the Port Arthur courthouse. It provided a good view of the water, where the swelling tides made for exciting footage.

Some of the national reporters tended to sensationalize the storm, Jordan said, exaggerating wind speeds prior to the storm. Shepherd Smith had a wind gauge and knew what the wind speeds were, so he was accurate.

Deadlines and nerves got the best of some, Jordan said. "At one point, Geraldo's people told us to move. I said, excuse me? Because you're national you're going to come in here and push us around? I've been helping you all night. That's not right. You can *ask* us to move."

Greg Bostwick, who was watching the national reporting while sheltered at the Edison Plaza building in downtown Beaumont, agreed that some reports were sensationalized.

"We were watching some of the Houston stations on cable. They were simulcasting from Galveston. They would position reporters at the corners of buildings where the air sucks around the building at twice the velocity anywhere else, producing 50 mph winds where they could barely stand up. It added sound effects and made it look better."

The tendency to "one-up" other media doesn't serve the public, Bostwick said, and one day will have disastrous results.

"You are getting people in the news media, particularly on the TV side where video is such a big, compelling story, into a situation where, I am convinced, one of these days we are going to see someone killed on live television by a flying missile of some kind. We're pushing the envelope here and we're sending mixed messages. We are saying you need to get out of this storm because it's so dangerous, but we as media don't listen to that. We're getting in the middle of it. It's crazy."

Bostwick admitted that in the competitive atmosphere, his station wasn't immune to chasing a story.

"We did something very foolish ourselves during Rita. At 10 o'clock that night, when the winds were 70 mph or a little higher, we were on the third or fourth floor of Edison Plaza looking out the window and (anchor) Dan Gresham said, 'Oh, there's Shepard Smith. You have got to go out there and talk to him.' I said, Dan, I 'm so unprepared for this hurricane it's stupid. I don't even have a toothbrush with me. I don't have a change of clothes. As soon as I walk outside I will be soaked to the bone."

Gresham said, "Nope, nope, I've got a little raincoat. You are going out there."

"So, like an idiot, I go out in this thing," Bostwick said. "The winds are so strong that (station reporter) Sally McDonald literally rolls down the street. We had to go grab her. I'm a pretty good-sized guy. I weigh about 200 pounds and I could hardly stand up. It took every bit of force I could manage leaning my body into the wind to walk.

"We finally get over to Shepard Smith, who was a little protected by his truck, and do this silly interview on national television. It was kind of neat to do. I'll grant you that. But when we returned to Edison Plaza, as we approached Entergy's door, there was an electronic sign at ground level. Just as we walked past it, a big gust of wind ripped that sign apart and a big piece of metal siding about 10 foot long broke away and crashed into the windows and shattered them.

"I told Dan we could have been hit by that and killed instantly. It's an example of how foolish you can be if you're not thinking straight. And apparently we didn't learn enough during Rita, because we almost got into trouble with Ike. During the height of the storm, we sent some people down to the seawall to see how high the water was. There was debris flying around and we had people outside in 100 mph wind. That is insane."

After those episodes, KFDM's management instituted a policy that states they will never again endanger reporter crews and anchors in a hurricane.

Around at 8 pm, Jordan parked in the Central Mall parking lot in Port Arthur and watched the blue light of transformers as they popped.

"Let me tell you something about Southeast Texas. When the lights are out, it's black. Even the refinery lights were out. You don't know where anything is. When I was coming back to the office around 11:30, the water was already up. The rain was bad and the winds were horrible. I was driving my truck and was concerned that the water would get over the roads. I know the area but I didn't want to make some stupid mistake and end up in the canal by misjudging a road because it was hard to see."

At the office, Jordan hooked up the generator so he could use the computer and charge the phones. There was enough power to run a light and a fan. He spoke to some people on the phone and listened to radio reports. By 1 a.m., he was "flat bored."

The front door had been locked and buttressed with newspapers inside and out. Jordan needed something from his truck so he went to the back door, being careful to keep his keys in his pocket. Sure enough, once he was outside, the wind caught the door and slammed it shut.

Problem was, he had no key to the back door. As he went to get inside his truck, which he had pulled within a foot of the building for protection, the wind caught the door and pinned his arm between the truck and the wall.

"Dumb butt me, I'm lucky I didn't break my arm," he said. "It was black and blue and hurt for weeks."

At that point, Jordan thought, "Well, what am I going to do? Its 2 o'clock and I'm locked out of the building. So I get in my truck and start to drive around town. Not the brightest thing in the world to do. I didn't make it very far. I am afraid of electricity but I didn't see any arcing. I went down to Calder Avenue, then realized that was a bad option, circled back around and came back and parked my truck. So now I'm thinking, how am I going to get into the building? At this point I am panicking. I know the front is boarded up. So I went and ripped away all the stuff we had stacked at the front door, shoved it aside and climbed over stacks of paper inside to get in."

In retrospect, he said, he never should have left.

By 4 a.m. Kirbyville was taking the brunt of the storm and his wife was "freaking out," Jordan said.

"She was sitting against the back wall of the brick house and said she could feel it moving. I am here and she is there. I don't want anything to happen to her, but I also have a job to do – and she knew that."

Jordan had boarded up all the windows to protect them. During the storm, a piece of plywood he had nailed against the shutters caught the wind and blew off in the yard. His wife went outside and grabbed the board with shutters still attached. A gust of wind grabbed it and for a moment, she thought she was going airborne.

"It pinned her against the wall, and it took her a little time to her to figure out how to get the board off her. She let it go and watched it fly past her," Jordan said.

While Jordan aggressively chases stories, he thinks the media – himself included – need to ask as tough questions of themselves as they do others.

"I learned that we don't work as well together as we all think we do. I try to work with everybody. Yeah, we've got the competition between us and The Enterprise, so most of my relationships obviously are with TV and radio people. At some point in time, it's not a competition any more. I think I am the hardest-edged newsperson in this town. I really do. I want to be first. I want to break the big story. But at some point it's not about being first. It's about helping people.

"We can do more to help people prepare. Learn from the mistakes. Try to be that information source for them. Step up. Find out all of the information instead of rushing. There was some bad information that went out. We need to be more careful about that, not just for us as a profession, but for the people. We owe it to them to make sure we are right, not first."

At the time, The Examiner's website wasn't great, Jordan said, but they posted as much as they could.

"We partnered a lot with (Beaumont radio station) KLVI. Those guys did a hell of a job, and we would do interviews and whatever we could to help them get the word out. Our websites were linked, and we were putting up photos and updating it the best we could. Our website went down for several days, which will never, ever happen again."

Al Caldwell had been on the air for 50 years when Rita hit. Needless to say, it wasn't his first rodeo.

Caldwell, along with a couple of sales people and on-air personalities Jack Pieper, Harold Mann, Jim Love, Neil Harrison, Don Rivers and Mickey Ashworth, stayed at KLVI during the storm. Their building is like a fortress, Caldwell said, and had no damage. They were well prepared with a 50 K generator, so they had a completely functioning studio. They slept for a few hours at a time on mattresses on the floor, taking turns working the phones and being on air.

Caldwell said the station learned from the damage done back in 1986 by Hurricane Bonnie, a weak Category 1, that it, as well as the public, wasn't prepared.

"We hadn't had a major hurricane in many years. We found out during Bonnie that the best way we could serve the public was to open the lines and let the people give us information. I told my guys, 'This is where we need to do this. The people can give us more information because of cell phone. They can give reports from where they are, including road conditions.'"

The challenge was making sure the reports were accurate.

"As primitive as it sounds, many times when we got people on the air, we asked, 'What is your source?'"

"Well, I just know."

"Tell me how you know and where you are," Caldwell would ask.

Every chance they got, the station would broadcast interviews with law enforcement officers, mayors, city council members, county commissioners, and other officials who were in a better position to have correct details.

KFDM Channel 6, KLVI's next-door neighbor, was knocked off the air. KLVI opened up its studios to them and all the other television stations so they could use computers to post online. They also hosted other media.

When The Beaumont Enterprise printed its first post-storm edition, KLVI broadcast that information so people could pick a copy up at drop-off sites.

"What The Enterprise had that we didn't was pictures. They were memory makers. Once we said something on the air, poof! it was gone. They did a fabulous job of documenting the storm for history, especially with the book they published."

While running down stories and interviewing people was tiring, the biggest challenge for the KLVI team was remaining patience with a severely-stressed and often rude public, Caldwell said.

"We were grateful for the generosity of people who called and the information they provided. But a lot of people were understandably frustrated. They couldn't get power, couldn't get to their house, and couldn't get gas or water. Every time we announced someone had 10,000 bags of ice, it was gone by the time they got there. They would call and say, 'Man, you sent us there and they didn't have any ice.'

"People have a propensity for not being able to understand they aren't the only ones in need. The people who were quickest got there first. And they would say, 'I've been trying to get you on the phone for three days. I can't get through.' After Rita, I told people that when I was stranded in Italy on 9/11, my phone bill back to the U.S. was $900. I would be on hold for six or seven hours with Continental Airlines trying to get through. With Rita, you had all of these people trying to get the same supplies."

After Rita, KLVI's oft-repeated message to the public was "If another storm ever comes this way, for God's sake, be prepared. Be sure you have water and food."

Caldwell said he thinks television and newspapers did a great job prior to Rita providing ample warnings and complete and accurate information.

"What people learned in Rita that they used in Ike is they paid attention to the media and the information they gave. And when they did get back on the air and printing again, the media did a lot to help people's morale. A lot of people were depressed and under a lot of stress."

Jack Pieper had been in radio since 1961. Rita, he said, was the defining story of his career.

"We did cover the ice storm in 1997, which had some similarities, but it was nothing like Rita. I was on the air for 21 days straight, as were most of us. We took three-hour on-air shifts in rotation."

Harold Mann was news director for the station, and did an outstanding job. Everyone pitched in to gather and disseminate news, including the music jocks, Pieper said.

The station's staff sat down with owner Clear Channel Communications prior to the storm to formulate their plan, which was how to best use their people, what sources to use for interviews, and how to make sure they had adequate supplies such as a generator, food and other supplies.

"We got a lot of people involved in the process and it worked well. It was the administration at Clear Channel that put it together and stepped up to the plate in furnishing everything we needed. It's a plan that can still be used today. We were able to cope with everything that arose."

Because KLVI was streaming live over the Internet, they received calls from media all across the U.S.

"We were, essentially, on-the-scene reporters."

Pieper remembers one call in particular that reflected the kindness of strangers.

"We had a group of Chicago firemen listening to us. We didn't know that until later, when they took up a collection and sent it to us. That was amazing."

The question-and-answer sessions with area law enforcement and politicians reassured the community that government still was functioning, Pieper said.

"I've been in this market for a long time and for years after Rita, people would approach me on the street and tell me how reassuring it was to hear my voice on the air. We were a security blanket for people who had no place else to go."

Each day was a repetitive process of taking calls and trying to get answers to questions they often had to turn back to the public, Pieper said.

"Almost everything was shut down. We had requests for veterinarians, banks, and pharmacists, for example. If you couldn't give someone an answer, that was frustrating. You put it out and hoped someone would hear and call you with an answer. We would add all those numbers and resources to our list."

For KLVI's staff, the storm was a serious, intense effort, like the 2 a.m. phone call to Jim Love from a family trapped in their house. The station contacted the appropriate emergency response team and directed them to the house.

There also were moments of levity.

"One of the nicest things that occurred on my watch was Zona Jones, the Beaumont attorney and county western singer, who came on the air and announced that he was giving away ice. It was a precious commodity. He drove over to Concord Road and handed it out for two days in a row. Before he left, he sang a song for us on the air. It was a lighthearted moment that made us come alive. There wasn't a lot to laugh about, but that was a moment of levity."

For Pieper, the sense of attending to the community's welfare made everything worthwhile.

"When it was all over, we had some time to reflect. You felt like you contributed something. We've been in this business a long time, but as a broadcaster, you knew you were doing something very important that had lasting impact."

Editor Roger Cowles had a simple plan for his newspaper, the Port Arthur News: everyone would evacuate, take care of themselves and their families and check back in as soon as possible.

"If a mandatory evacuation was called, we planned to follow the rules," he said.

Cowles, who was born in Groves and had lived in Southeast Texas all his life, remembers his family evacuating for Hurricane Carla in 1961. Carla hit near Port Lavaca, which kept Southeast Texas from suffering the brunt of the storm.

When Rita began her turn toward Southeast Texas, the paper bought a supply of food and water and stacked it in the conference room. That was about as much preparation as they knew to make.

Cowles made sure his parents had left for their lake home in Ivanhoe, about seven miles south of Woodville. "We thought that was far enough to be safe," he laughed. "Little did I know."

Cowles' plan was to tell the stories of people who didn't have a way out and were trying to find one. He interviewed evacuees at the Beaumont Civic Center who were waiting to board buses. He drove to the Southeast Texas Regional Airport in Nederland and watched the military unload tons of food and water before filling the planes with medical special needs folks and flying them to safety.

His last stop was the Elegante Hotel in Beaumont where officials had gathered to hold press briefings about what steps the government and area industry would take next.

About mid-day Friday, he went back to the paper, wrote stories and filed them with Community Newspaper Holdings, Inc. (CNHI), a news service co-op in Birmingham, Ala. that owns the News. Because the News wasn't printing that night, it was the only way Cowles could report news in hopes his readers would have access somehow.

"The Internet wasn't quite as developed then, at least our ability to use it. We did have a webpage up and running. Town News hosted our website so we couldn't directly put things on our site. We had to send PDFs in."

Back then, the News wasn't using the Internet the way it does now with breaking news and up to the minute updates, Cowles said.

Late that afternoon, when he finished filing his stories, Cowles went home to make sure his house was secured. He and his son, Ben, who was a high school senior at the time, and his daughter, Katy, who was in college, caravanned to Ivanhoe.

It was dusk and hardly anyone still was left on the road in Groves. The other side of Kountze, they caught up with the tail end of the evacuation nightmare. The state had just initiated contraflow, turning both sides of the highway into one-way flow north.

"People were just taking over the roads. Local people tried to go south against the flow in Hardin County, heading into five lanes of oncoming traffic. We got to experience that all the way up to Ivanhoe," Cowles said.

At the camp house, the family tried to keep up with what was happening by watching TV. They went to bed sometime around midnight. At 3 a.m. a big "thunk" shook the house. The top of a pine tree had snapped off and driven like an arrow into the roof.

"That pretty much got everybody up," Cowles said.

Cowles, who was a smoker at the time, went outside and stood in gale-force winds and watched the winds blowing sideways as he pulled on a cigarette. He looked next door and saw that a tree had crunched the house. He and his dad went to check on the family.

"They were scared to death," Cowles said. "We brought them to our house. That was our introduction to what was about to happen."

When the storm had passed, Cowles discovered his family had lost three vehicles that sat in the driveway, crushed by trees. In a stroke of luck, Cowles had parked his car across the street in a large clearing.

"I had my file servers and computer in that car. One of the last things I did was load them into the car and take them with me. It would have been bad."

The wind raged until close to dawn. Cowles and his family went outside, walked around and found they were trapped by downed trees crossing the road.

"There was no leaving," he said. "We had brought a bunch of food, and my mom made a huge pot of spaghetti on her gas stove and fed the neighborhood."

After lunch, "throngs of people" showed up in the streets with chain saws and cut the downed trees into sections, loaded them on pickups and hauled them away, Cowles said. By early afternoon, the roads were passable.

Cowles and his son headed back to Groves to see if they could get the newspaper up and running. They encountered almost no vehicles on the road. When they came to the intersection of Twin City Highway and U.S. 69 by Lamar University, they hit their first DPS roadblock.

Cowles flashed the holograms that had been passed out to those critical to getting things back up and running, including media. He also dropped the judge's name. The trooper, who was not from the area, said, "Who is Carl Griffith?

"I said, 'He's the county judge. He signed this card.' It worked. He let us through."

After checking the newspaper, which had no visible damage, much to Cowles' relief, they drove around Groves checking on family members' homes. His home had lost a lot of shingles but fared well otherwise. Others in the area were not so lucky.

"We saw houses smashed by trees. We saw where tornadoes had hit and a house had just blown up. I never saw so many steeples in church yards in my life. We saw Groves city employees already working on clearing streets. It was a maze. You couldn't go from Point A to Point B – you'd inch along around blocks. We drove until we lost daylight."

Navigating the city was treacherous. In addition to the downed trees, limbs and power lines, pulverized leaves stripped from the trees covered everything with a green carpet. It was impossible to tell where a road ended and a ditch began.

Cowles' landline at home worked, so he called reporter Ashley Sanders, who had evacuated to her home town in Tyler. He fed her descriptions of what he saw: the Methodist church with a huge hole in the ceiling, canopies from a Texaco station in the middle of the highway, buildings destroyed.

Sanders wrote the stories Cowles reported but couldn't post to the paper's website. She discovered that she could post on the comments section of their home page.

"It wasn't in a real visible place, but people found it in amazing numbers on Saturday night. We used that for all our stories," Cowles said.

Posting to the forum, called "Hey Martha," had an impact on how she would develop as a journalist, Sanders, now managing editor of news at The Beaumont Enterprise, said.

"We created such a unique and emotional connection to our readers. They would ask me through their posts if Roger had checked on their neighborhood or if he would mind popping in at their house to see if their cat was OK. People were so desperate for news from home and no one had prepared to be gone so long. The forum became more than just a bulletin board for news stories. It really became a digital conversation between perfect strangers, some of whom were willing to have a sibling or cousin who did not evacuate check on a specific location mentioned in a post and report back. It was journalism at its purest and sincerely inspired me to be a better reporter and neighbor."

On Sunday, CNHI sent in a truck and trailer and huge generator so the News could become operational again. By that time, photographers Mike Tobias and Guiseppe Barranco were back, as were several department heads. They headed out and covered the news, making a stop at the Holiday Inn in Port Arthur, where the city had set up its emergency operations center.

The limited staff produced its first print edition after the storm on Monday for Tuesday delivery.

"I had to send Mike Tobias to be the production department. He had never laid out a newspaper but he was selected to go – and he learned how to put a newspaper together," Cowles said.

The staff emailed their stories and photos Barranco had shot to Tobias, who had been sent to their sister paper, the Huntsville Item. They put together an eight-page paper, printed in Huntsville and trucked down to South and Mid-County.

The Beaumont Enterprise, a Hearst Corporation daily newspaper that serves Southeast Texas, was facing its own challenges. Like other media outlets, it wasn't prepared for the aftermath of a major hurricane.

Brian Pearson, Managing Editor for News for The Enterprise, had been at the paper since 2001 so it was his first hurricane as a member of the media. And what a hurricane it was.

"I remember there was a lot of fear after Katrina and seeing what it did to New Orleans. We had pretty much decided if it was a Category 4 or above we would consider evacuating. If it was 3 or below, we would stay," said Pearson, now managing editor of the Tyler Morning Telegraph.

Employees were given the option of evacuating with their families or staying and working the storm and its aftermath. Many reporters stayed, along with the photo staff and the newsroom management of Publisher Aubrey Webb, Editor Tim Kelly, Managing Editor Ron Franscell, and Pearson. Other reporters evacuated to Dallas and San Antonio. A photo and reporter team moved north with the evacuation to report on their experiences. As soon as the storm was over, those reporters and copy desk staff gathered together to report and file stories from where they were. A group of six worked out of the Dallas Morning News, which generously offered them space. They interviewed evacuees and made phone calls gathering information to file stories via computer. Other reporters drove to East Texas and chronicled the evacuation and sheltering of evacuees.

The team decided The Enterprise building, a three-story structure, was as good a place as any in which to shelter. They later would wonder if that had been the best choice.

The staff stocked up on water and food, as well as flashlights and other supplies. What they didn't have was backup power. At one point, the Houston Chronicle, a sister paper, sent a generator, but it was much too powerful to use at The Enterprise, Pearson said.

"It would have fried the press."

The editorial staff started the night on the third floor in the newsroom. As the storm grew stronger it blew the roof covering off and water began raining in. The old ceiling tiles became saturated and crumbled onto the floor in blood red pools of rusty water. The windows bowed in, looking as if they were going to explode at any moment, Pearson said. At one point, he walked down a hallway and heard a huge crash behind him. The rooftop air-conditioning unit had fallen through the roof and landed where he had just been standing.

The staff moved down to the second floor. While some eventually slept, Pearson was too cranked up. He and several others took lawn chairs and parked them in the mouth of the lower-level concrete parking garage and watched the show.

"We felt safe there. We watched transformers blow and the building façade across the street come crashing down. It was crazy, like being at the end of a power wand in the car wash. We didn't have any power and there wasn't anything we could do, so we watched this awesome thing play out in front of us. It was a constant roar punctuated by intense gusts that would last 15 seconds or more. They came in waves and the next gusts would be at a higher intensity. Between 3:45 and 4 a.m. we got the most intense, huge blast."

News Reporter Jacqui Lane spent the night next door at Entergy, covering the EOC. She watched the air conditioner and the roof peel away and was worried about the rest of the staff.

"She thought we might all be dead," Pearson said.

Reporter Kevin Dwyer spent the night on the Cape Vincent so he would be able to roll out with the first responders the next day.

At the paper, Pearson was struggling with the logistics of coverage under extremely adverse conditions.

"It was tough to get a handle on what to report on. It was a target rich environment for news stories. It was pretty overwhelming," Pearson said. "Kevin came back, and he and I went out to survey the damage."

Because The Enterprise had no power, Ron Franscell was coordinating setting up the copy desk staff at the Chronicle in Houston while Pearson coordinated news coverage, assigning stories and editing copy. Someone had the idea of hooking up their laptops to car batteries. It worked. The reporters came back from the field, took turns typing up their stories and sent them to the Chronicle over telephone land lines that were working.

Within six hours, they had filed their first stories, which they placed on The Enterprise' website.

"We were thinking of people out there in places like Dallas or San Antonio who were wondering what had happened here and wondering what emergency officials were saying? The main thing was to advise people, don't come back yet. If I'm an evacuee and I'm worried about my home, I want to come see it. It was important that they realized conditions were unlivable unless you were very well prepared. There was a certain level of chaos going on."

Reporters continued to file stories all day and late into the night, including a running list of damage to grocery stores, restaurants and businesses on down to neighborhood damage. They filed as many photos as they could shoot and upload so people could see for themselves what had happened in Southeast Texas. They also kept tabs on restoration efforts, from power resumption to debris removal.

"It took me a good day or two to get a plan in place. We were working 18-20 hours a day to generate as much information as possible. At one point I realized we couldn't go on like that because it would burn the staff out. We divided up into beats and I told them, file one main story and one sidebar. That's all you're going to do today. I sensed a great deal of relief. Journalists want to cover everything, but you just can't. We were learning on the fly. Once we got everything into the system and we got beats assigned it got a lot easier in a hurry."

Their efforts didn't go unnoticed.

"We had overwhelming positive feedback from the community. We had no idea who was looking at our stuff, but we learned people were on it all the time. We got more hits than ever before. We provided a comprehensive look at what was going on. People said their decision not to come back came from reading our website and the warnings we issued. It was a very grateful public."

Pearson got to experience that first hand when the paper published for the first time on Sunday, October 2. The staff had been building a newspaper every day, putting it in PDF form. On that Sunday, The Enterprise published a Special Edition, "Comeback Time," which included all the previous days' unpublished papers.

"We printed the paper in Houston, and the staff went out and handed out newspapers for free. I loaded up my car and drove around neighborhoods. There was a big car line at the mall about a mile long of people waiting for ice, water and supplies. One of my high points was driving along the line and handing out newspapers to people sitting in their cars. I've never seen people so excited to get a newspaper. That was fun, finally getting a paper into their hands and seeing the looks on their faces."

Like everyone else trying to manage more than their own lives, Pearson learned some valuable lessons.

"From a management perspective, I made my share of mistakes. There were times my temper was tested. I had to learn how to be calmer in a storm, realizing that in addition to driving the news, I had the responsibility to take care of our people and their well-being. It made me realize there is only so much we can do in a day and we couldn't get to it all. It was getting to be a fairly serious health issue.

"I also realized that that staff was the best staff I could possibly have. I'd put them up against any staff anywhere. They gave it everything they had and did an outstanding job. I was very proud of the way they handled themselves. It's like we were a big family united behind a common cause. It was an adventure, but a very stressful one."

When KBTV-12 managers saw Hurricane Rita continue to strengthen, they decided their hurricane action plan needed altering. Initially, said Chief Engineer Mark Cormier, the plan had a list of who would evacuate and who would stay to keep the station up and running. Those who stayed were assigned such tasks as picking up supplies, cash, food and water and other things needed during a hurricane.

When they saw that Rita had been ungraded to a Category 5 storm, the owner decided to evacuate the steel siding building because he wasn't sure it would survive that level of stress.

Thursday afternoon, Cormier linked to television station KTKR, a

Houston area ABC affiliate that uplinked KBTV via satellite feed. At 6 p.m. he locked the doors and headed to a relative's house in DeRidder, La.

"To my knowledge, everybody left town," Cormier said. "One of my engineers, Glen Emenhiser, stayed at his home in Winnie and watched television through an antenna. Glen said we went off the air at 2 a.m. Saturday morning."

Although the station had a generator at the transmitter site, it ran out of fuel. The system required pumping the day tank full when it emptied, and no one was there to do that. The station has since remedied that problem with automatic generators.

Cormier left DeRidder at 10 a.m. Saturday in a borrowed vehicle, since his was "holding up a carport." He worked his way around downed trees and power lines by driving through ditches or waiting for someone with a chain saw to cut a path. The station has a chain saw, but it was stored at the transmitter site.

His first stop was at the transmitter site, where he had to walk through the woods because the roads were impassable. He inspected the building and found all the equipment was functional, but there was no need to start the generator back up because there was no signal coming from the studio in Beaumont. By 3:30 that afternoon, Cormier had made his way back to the station.

"When I got here, I was the only one here. At that point, I retrieved my 44 magnum from the truck and entered the building because I didn't know what to expect," he said. "Although the plywood stayed up, the roof covering was gone so it rained in. All of the ceiling tile was on the floor and water was everywhere. The only part of the building that didn't sustain damage was the sales and general manager offices. My office was at that end of the hall so it was OK. But the master control, news department, production control, engineering shop – all sustained considerable damage."

Cormier put together a list of what he would need to get the station back on the air. At that point his general manager was back, and they decided that since curfew was approaching and they had to be off the streets, they would get an early start Sunday morning.

"Beaumont police were in no mood for people messing around," he said.

On Sunday, the team got a small switcher and audio board put together and was able to get some programming through some of their other sources, a studio camera, and the ABC network.

"At that point another engineer who once was my boss came over from KHOU in Houston and we went back to the transmitter site to repair it and get it started again. At 2:33 Sunday afternoon, I signed the station back on the air with ABC network. I had told my manager I would have us back on the air at 2. I lied."

As far as he knows, Cormier said, the only other local broadcasting at that point was a couple of radio stations.

"By that time, Glen had come back. Later that afternoon, Meteorologist Patrick Vaughan was back and doing interviews. We knew we needed to get on the air and disseminate as much info as we could. We decided to go live in the studio with just Patrick Vaughan and general manager Mike Elrod. Patrick gave out his cell phone number, and it started ringing continuously. My hat is off to him. He did an outstanding job. It was amazing how many people were out there watching on battery power or generators at their home. We stayed on the air like that until midnight. By then we had the news director back and we were trying to find out as much information from civil defense guys and other officials who had information to share. We called it a day, went home, started at it again Monday."

By Monday, Cormier had set up a streaming feed from the studio to the Internet.

"The folks who were staying in places like Tyler would get on their computers and shut down the network on the hotel because so many people were watching our streaming feed. Once they did that, nobody got to see anything."

By that time, Cormier had turned his attention to turning the station into something that could be a workable building again.

"About 90 percent of my broadcasting equipment was destroyed. It took a lot of Southern technology to get back on the air. We stayed on the air giving out information for the next six or seven days. Programming was either ABC network or local coverage. We weren't back to normal schedule. People wanted to buy commercial time. They had supplies they wanted to sell. But our commercial playback ability was not available. What we would do is pass on the information, like M&D would be open from these hours to these hours and only one person at a time could come in. Home Depot was doing that do. We gave information on points of distribution for water and ice and businesses that were open on a limited basis where people could get food, building materials and all the stuff coming from the EOC at Ford Park. We had them on every day."

The station restored normal programming and commercials about two weeks later.

At his home, Cormier was without power for 17 days, but he had enough generator power to operate two refrigerators, lights, the television and a small window air conditioning unit so he could sleep at night.

"We had five or six employees sleeping in the sales department because they had no place to go. They had no power, and they were here working. Before the hurricane, we had gone out and bought a freezer and a bunch of food and gas so we could have fuel in our cars. Everything was destroyed from Lake Charles to Beaumont, so Houston was our lifeline. We were driving every night over that way and buying gasoline."

It took the station until March 2008 to finish rebuilding the station and go live with its new control room. The master control and equipment area now is protected beneath a false ceiling that sits below a vaulted ceiling sprayed with water-repelling foam.

"If it ever rains in on me again my equipment will stay dry so we can remain on the air. And we have new generators – one here and one at the transmitter. "

Cormier said as difficult as it was coping with what had to be done to become functional enough to deliver the news to those who need it, he understood that it's just part of life.

"You deal with it, and you move on. You can't let it get you down. It's just, well, this is broke, so fix it."

Chapter Seven

Emergency Operations Centers

Although Rita had been downgraded to a strong Cat- egory 3 hurricane by the time she came ashore, she was a monstrous Category 5 when authorities had to make their evacuation decisions. Reconnaissance photos captured a storm whose circular bands filled the entire Gulf of Mexico, something unseen before by those in the region. It was a frightening sight, to say the least. Her intensity, coupled with the damages the smaller and less-powerful Hurricane Katrina had brought, created an unprecedented fear and awareness of what might happen.

The storm surge alone was projected to be as much as 20 feet, which could mean significant flooding for much of the region. It was not unreasonable to believe hundreds of thousands of homes would be uninhabitable ... if still standing. The death toll from drowning could be significant.

Those who had evacuated could do nothing but watch dramatic accounts of newscasters barely able to withstand the winds or standing in a foot of water as they described the intensity of the storm. Those in shelters across the region that had lost power could only listen to radio stations on their battery-operated radios or pass along reports from people talking to friends who had stayed behind. Many of those reports turned out to be rumor, but it would be more than a day or two of anxiety before the truth came out.

For years, the City of Beaumont's Emergency Management Plan had called for emergency response teams to shelter in place at the Beaumont Fire Department's main station in downtown Beaumont. The two-story brick building houses the Fire Museum of Texas on the bottom floor and offices on the second floor.

When Entergy Texas, the electrical power provider for the region, offered its headquarters as a shelter, the county and city gratefully accepted. Edison Plaza, often referred to as the Entergy building, sits on a bluff on the banks of the Neches River. At 17 floors, it anchors the city's skyline.

The structure was built and owned by Gulf States Utilities, Entergy Texas' predecessor. The building eventually was sold, and Entergy was there on a 25-year lease. Due to a downturn in the economy, the building had several vacant floors, so Entergy Texas President and CEO Joe Domino made the offer, thinking it would be beneficial if all first responders were gathered in one place.

Entergy's emergency management plan called for its key executives and staff to evacuate to an alternate operations center in Conroe during a Category 4 or 5 hurricane. As Rita approached, Domino was given the option to follow that plan or to stay in Beaumont. Domino checked into the building's design and was assured it would withstand 130 mile per hour winds.

"I felt pretty confident we would be safe. For double insurance, I made sure those who were spending the night in the building were not sleeping under a window. Safety always is a primary concern for us."

Although the structural integrity of the building provided a safe place for first responders, it had its limitations. The building had an emergency generator that was put into operation back in the 1970s, but it had limited capability. Power was designated primarily for the 12th floor where the computers are located. It also powered an emergency elevator and lighting for two floors deemed critical in an emergency.

Beaumont Fire Department Captain Pat Grimes spent a lot of time monitoring the storm from the fifth floor windows, where Beaumont firefighters and EMS crews spent the night. Grimes had brought his own cot, pillow, blanket and a flashlight. He bunked with around 200 or so others in one big open room, with the small EOC conference room in the center. A bare bulb on a tall lamp provided the only light in the EOC, where all the available power was used to operate computers and communication equipment.

The Beaumont Foundation, one of Beaumont attorney Wayne Reaud's philanthropic outreaches, made setting up the EOC easier. The foundation supplies computers to help underserved students in the U.S. When the foundation's President Frank Newton heard about the EOC at Entergy, he called and asked first responders, "Can you use any computers?"

"Boy, can we," they answered. How fast can you get them over here?"

The foundation provided all the computers they had in stock and then called their supplier and had more shipped in, still in the boxes.

"The computers got lots of use," Newton said. "They were a welcome addition."

After Rita recovery, 80 percent of the computers went on to be redistributed to students.

Once the EOC crew got everything as much in place as they could, they went down to Entergy's cafeteria and shared a good steak dinner. For Grimes, it was surreal, trying to absorb the magnitude of what happened with the evacuation of Katrina, coupled with the anticipation of what was about to happen.

"It was overwhelming just watching the power of the storm once the wind started blowing. You watch the transformers explode and lights going out around 8 or 9 o'clock until there were no lights at all. Around midnight, things really started getting loud. You're listening to the building creak as it moves with the wind. This thing goes on for one hour, then two, then six. I was thinking there is not going to be anything left standing. It was such an awesome power," Grimes said.

The EMS had set up an operation for tetanus shots on the sixth floor, and City Health Department Director Ingrid Holmes was running that.

Everything they knew to do, they had done. They had put in the paperwork requesting everything they thought they would need, from portapotties and generators to food and water.

Grimes and the others lay down to try to get some sleep, knowing they needed the rest before the next phase hit. Sleep was impossible, especially as the storm intensified.

"I didn't sleep at all. I remember listening to the sounds and realizing what the wind could do to this big old building," Grimes said.

Across the street at the Beaumont Fire Department Headquarters, the communications center took calls all night long. People kept calling saying they wanted to get out and needed help. By that time, it was too late. All officials could do was make a list of those who wanted to evacuate and tell them they would go check on them in the morning.

"There was nothing else we could do," Grimes said. "We also had a couple of calls for houses on fire, but we had no choice but to let them burn."

During the storm, the hundreds of windows in the building held strong, as promised. The building lost four windows, two on the executive floor and two on the ground floor in the cafeteria, which was not designed with the same structural integrity as the rest of the building, Domino said.

"There is some debate on whether they blew out or whether a sign blew into them. It might have happened at the same time. I don't know," Domino said.

By the time the storm hit, close to 600 people had taken shelter there, including essential Entergy employees, the Beaumont Fire Department, paramedics, area elected officials, government officials and a group from the national media, as well as local reporters.

The thick darkness made it impossible to know how much damage the hurricane's winds were causing. The longer the night went, the more anxiety grew.

Entergy's engineers were tracking damage to the electrical transmission system for the region through a SCADE remote monitoring system of the company's sub stations. One by one, they saw them trip offline. It was not a good sign.

"We knew there was a lot of damage out there. We just didn't know how much," Entergy's Director of Customer Service Vernon Pierce said.

Domino sent his children out of town, but he and his wife, Linda, stayed in the building with his crew and slept on the floor. Like everyone else, he worried about what the storm would do to his home.

"I had no idea whether I would even see a house when I went back," he said.

Linda, who is active in the Roman Catholic Church, brought Bishop Curtis Guillory of the Diocese of Beaumont in to conduct services the Sunday after the storm.

KFDM Meteorologist Greg Bostwick earned his stay, providing accurate information throughout the long night in the command center, which was filled with radio and communications equipment.

"Fortunately, we had internet capability so I was able to access radar images. We monitored the National Weather Service radar in Lake Charles to see where the storm was. That was huge to be able to get that information," he said.

At the first briefing of the evening at 7 p.m. someone spotted Bostwick and asked if he would tell them about the approaching storm. The weatherman said he could share at least a little bit of good news.

"By that time, it became obvious to me that the center of the storm was not going to come ashore in Texas, but just east of the Sabine over in Cameron Parish. I told them we would not see the catastrophic storm surge in Jefferson County like Cameron Parish (in Louisiana) was going to get – and that's exactly what happened. We did not get the 20-plus feet of water that Cameron Parish got."

Bostwick warned the group that Hurricane Rita still was a very large storm, and the winds would cause major damage.

"Obviously, if it had hit at the intensity it had at one time, which was about two days before landfall, there was extreme concern that it was going to be worse than Katrina. Whoever got it was going to be absolutely hammered. The storm surge would have been devastating."

During the night, Bostwick continued to look at any data he could access, from satellite pictures to reports from the National Hurricane Center, providing updates every five to seven minutes.

"Radar imagery was the most important," he said. "We could tell exactly when and where it would make landfall."

The biggest concern for Southeast Texas all along had been the storm surge, Bostwick said.

"It always is in our area because of our low elevation and the fact that the shallowness of the Gulf waters offshore can let the surge pile up to tremendous heights. We can get as large or larger of a storm surge here as anywhere in the Western Hemisphere."

The seawall in Port Arthur is the primary protection for South and Mid-County. If a storm surge is higher than the levee, the same wall that keeps the seawater out then traps all the water inside.

"Once the hurricane is over, you have a lake. The seawall acts like a reservoir or a dam. It is a horrific thing to overtop a levee system, as we witnessed in New Orleans."

The lowest point of an anxiety-filled night came at 3 a.m. when a man called from his cell phone to say he was trapped in his attic.

"Of course, the immediate conclusion is he's in his attic because the levee system has ruptured and the water is filling up his house. When we heard that call, our hearts sunk. We thought, the ultimate disaster we feared is unfolding now. The city of Port Arthur and Bridge City are flooding. All those places are going under water," Bostwick said.

It turned out the phone call was a cruel prank, but for a while, those who had stayed to help after the storm didn't know that. Needless to say, the jerk who made the call would be wise never to confess.

"I'd like to call him something else," Bostwick said.

When the storm knocked out the electrical company's power in the middle of the night, those inside were stuck in an airless building. Not only did it not have air-conditioning, but the walls of windows could not be opened.

Emergency responders would work in the sweltering heat for three days before more generators could be acquired and wired into the system to provide relief.

From inside the safety of the schools in Lumberton, first responders from Mid and South County could hear the merciless pounding of rain and the sharp cracking of huge, aged trees snapping like dry twigs. Electrical transformers crackled and exploded, scattering streamers of light for brief moments. Large shards of debris scratched against the pavement and clawed at anything in its way.

Imagination can carry those inside only so far. What did the blanket of darkness hide? Could the reality be worse than their fearful minds conjured?

As the storm passed over Lumberton, Port Arthur Police Chief Mark Blanton began second-guessing his decision to stay in Lumberton rather than taking his staff further north.

"I was standing outside, and I watched a portable building explode and saw a pine tree snap in two. At that point I was concerned that I had made a mistake in judgment. At one point, we had talked about going to Conroe. Our city government was there at Lumberton, confined in this building, and I was really worried. When the power went out and it got really bad and I started seeing the damage in Lumberton, I began to wonder if I had given a death sentence to my employees."

Hardin County Judge Billy Caraway knew once the storm was over he would have to make decisions that would impact the 50,000 citizens under his care. There had been no precedent on which he could base his plans; his county never had evacuated from a storm. As Rita assaulted the county courthouse in Kountze, he did his best to keep those around him calm.

"Everybody was scared. Really scared," he said.

Tired bodies had found any available place they could to rest. Some people slept in the hall and against the stairs. Such close quarters provided Caraway with an opportunity to lighten the mood.

"One woman was keeping everyone awake. She snored louder than anybody I'd ever seen," Caraway laughed. "I mean, it was unbelievable."

Caraway left his small, dark office, stood in the hall and made a loud announcement: "Everybody settle down. The crisis is over."

Confusion covered their faces. Crisis over? The storm clearly still was raging outside.

"She's turned over on her side, and she's not snoring anymore."

Jefferson County has around 2,000 or so emergency response workers, including law enforcement, firefighters, emergency medical service personnel and trained volunteers. Beaumont and the cities of South and Mid-County – Port Arthur, Nederland, Groves and Port Neches – each have their own police and fire departments. The Jefferson County Sheriff's Department handles law enforcement for the unincorporated areas while volunteers provide fire and EMS services.

When Beaumont and Jefferson County authorities chose not to go to Lumberton but to ride out the storm at the Entergy Building, they urged South and Mid-County to do the same. It led to some heated discussions.

"We got into arguments with the mayor of Port Arthur, but we got that cleared up," Curran said. "Then Judge Griffith had a difference of opinion and wanted us to go to Entergy. We had a little disagreement over that. He was concerned with the structural integrity of the school and our safety. I have a construction background, and I knew the school was built to code for 120 mph wind speed protection. They were fairly new structures, so I felt comfortable."

The discussions are "just part of the process," Curran said. "That was the other lesson we learned. If you've got a plan, stick to your plan. It worked like clockwork."

Most of Beaumont's first responders, including firefighters, had chosen to stay in the Entergy Building, while the majority of the police officers holed up at Christus St. Elizabeth Hospital, which had a sturdy, multi-level concrete parking garage. It became a favorite spot from which to watch the oncoming storm. Key staff from the City of Beaumont's 800 employees boarded the Cape Vincent with city vehicles and equipment to wait until the storm cleared.

Beaumont City Manager Kyle Hayes decided to stay in his office at

City Hall.

"I felt like the building was soundly built. It was a personal preference. In hindsight, the ship was probably much safer, but I didn't know that at the time," Hayes said.

Once the storm intensified, most of the media had taken cameras and rain-soaked bodies inside. A few daredevils, thumbing their noses in ignorance of what could happen, were running on adrenalin and ambition, not common sense.

Around midnight, Hayes' cell phone rang. It was Stephanie Flory, a friend who had evacuated with her family to Dallas and was watching CNN in hopes of learning how Southeast Texas was faring during the storm.

"Anderson Cooper is downstairs," she said. "Go let him in!"

Cooper was reporting live from the porte-cochère at Beaumont's City Hall, wedged between two large vehicles he was using as a wind shield. At the time, the unflappable news anchor was riding a wave of favorable attention from his emotional coverage of Hurricane Katrina. Cooper was faring much better than Fox News' Shepherd Smith, who was reporting from behind the Beaumont Enterprise building, directly in front of Entergy. At one point, a gust of wind caught Smith and sent him tumbling, much to the amusement of the more prudent first responders watching from the wall of windows inside the EOC at Edison Plaza.

Hayes and City Comptroller Todd Simoneaux, who also was spending the night at City Hall, went downstairs and tried to open the door to let Cooper in. It took all their strength to overcome the hurricane-force winds.

"Look," a sympathetic Hayes told Cooper. "I'm going to leave this door open so you can come in when you want to. There's a restroom down the hall." He shook hands with Cooper and his cameraman and went back upstairs.

Just 28 miles east on Interstate 10, the easternmost city in Texas also was bracing for Rita. Orange, the county seat of Orange County, is where the Sabine River separates Texas from Louisiana.

Shawn Oubre became the assistant city manager for Orange in February 2005 and assumed city manager responsibilities just before Rita. He worked closely with the mayor in planning for Hurricane Rita.

To be eligible for state and federal assistance, cities must file approved emergency management plans with the state. These plans outline how cities will address evacuation, shelter, traffic management and shutting down city services both individually and as part of a regional effort. If a city chooses not to have its own plan, it falls under the county plan, which is mandatory, Oubre said.

For Rita, Orange participated in a county/regional decision to call for an evacuation. The city split its personnel and equipment between the Orange County shelter at the National Guard Armory north of Interstate 10 and the Temple Inland plant to ensure it could get some equipment back to the city in a timely manner. The plan also kept the city from exposing all of its equipment and employees in one location.

The days leading up to Rita were filled with multiple meetings and conference calls that led to the decision to evacuate. The city had begun stocking up on essentials such as fuel, food, water, and other supplies days before Rita hit. The state sent buses to evacuate local citizens who didn't have transportation.

"It was a proud moment to view staff going beyond normal duties to assist local citizens," Oubre said. "I saw staff visit and console the elderly and people with special needs as they waited patiently for evacuation. The sadness of the moment was the realization that there were some people who did not have the means to take care of themselves. These people depended on total strangers to protect them from the disaster."

Once everyone was in place, they waited for the storm to hit, wondering just how bad it might be for a vulnerable, low-lying city. At a mere seven feet above sea level, Orange is susceptible to flooding.

"The night of the hurricane found power outages at the shelter and a generator failure. The outside was pitch dark with the howling of the wind and force of rain pounding the metal roof. We only hoped the building would withstand the hurricane with each sound of snapping pine trees. The sound was like cracking your knuckles and occurred steadily throughout the night," Oubre said.

"The dispatchers continued to receive calls that turned into pleas for help from residents that refused to evacuate but now regretted that decision. These pleas were to rescue them as trees had fallen through their roofs. Unable to help or rescue, dispatchers were only able to write down their address and check on them after the danger had passed."

For Oubre, the most stressful moment was a 2 a.m. conference call with the Lake Charles weather service, broadcast over the speakerphone on Orange Mayor Brown Claybar's cell phone.

"With landlines inoperable, elected and appointed officials sat quietly in a room as advisors warned of the backside of Rita approaching with the greatest winds to come. Nerves were on edge as the advisors admitted that the wind and rain might damage the building that we occupied. It was decided to skip the 4 a.m. conference call because we would be experiencing what we were discussing. We decided to call back at 6 when the hurricane should have passed over Orange County. It was the first time that some would wonder if we would survive."

At St. Elizabeth Hospital in Beaumont, Mary Egan had done all she could prior to the storm and was as comfortable with her decision for the staff to stay with the remaining 128 patients as she could be under the circumstances.

St. Elizabeth was built in the 1960s as a nuclear shelter, Egan said.

"Thanks to the good nuns, St. E. is built like a fortress. We thought, OK, we'll do well here."

The stories coming out of New Orleans about patients dying alone in flooded hospitals during Hurricane Katrina had horrified Egan.

"Because we are a faith-based organization, life to us is sacred. People who work here want to work here because they know they are a part of the human ministry of Christ. I was bound and determined we were not going to have a Katrina here. No way. We would not have patients left alone and dying. If it did happen, I would be dead along with them," Egan said.

Egan had the staff move all patients on the window side of the hospital to the inside corridors of the hospital. They stayed with the patients, waiting for the storm to hit and praying the hospital held its own against the wind and water.

Around 2 a.m. Saturday they lost power but the emergency generators kicked in. Things were going as well as could be expected until 5 a.m. when the hospital lost the one thing it could not do without: water.

"Something happened to the water system that caused the city to shut it down. I knew I could do without power. There were potty bags and all that. But there was no way we could provide patient care in terms of safety and sanitary conditions. I knew at that point we had to get the 128 patients out."

Egan notified Christus president Dr. Tom Royer, who made arrangements to move the patients to a sister hospitals St. Joseph and St. Catherine in Houston and St John in Nassau Bay.

The next obstacle was ambulances. Egan called Judge Griffith, who asked her how many ambulances she needed. She told him to send 90.

"Carl worked his magic and got us the ambulances. Within hours, all of a sudden you see all the ambulances driving up in a parade from Houston. I'm out there counting the ambulances, and they only sent me 55. So I got back on the phone and said, 'I need 90.'"

She got them.

Dr. Aiyandar Bharati, chief of neonatology, loaded four babies from the neonatal intensive care unit in two ambulances, accompanied by nurses. He drove the mothers to Houston, so they would be with their babies.

Egan approached her nursing staff and told them they could get the patients out, but she needed somebody to go with them so they didn't feel abandoned.

Thirty-five nurses volunteered to go, along with pharmacists, respiratory therapists and physical therapists to help with the lifting. The patients went by ambulance while the staff took two buses.

"Fortunately, I have wonderful, wonderful nurses. They all took one step forward and said, 'We'll go.' I don't think I was ever so proud of staff in my entire life. It was phenomenal."

Chapter Eight

Coming Home

Citizens who had left endured a grueling and at times
life-threatening trip. Many ended up at designed shelters in cities that suffered major damages of their own, including loss of power, then had to
evacuate a second time. Once they found a place to stay until the evacuation order was lifted and they could go home, they could do little more
than wait to hear how bad the damages were. That proved much harder
than anticipated. Cell phone communication was hampered loss of towers. Many land lines were useless because of downed telephone lines.

Many of those who stayed regretted their decision and took advantage of the transportation services offered by the cities and counties and
evacuated after the storm. Those who remained in place tried to work
their way across the downed power lines and debris-filled streets to
check on relatives' and friends' homes. The ones who could get through
did their best to pass on the information.

City water and sewer were down. Those with water wells were in no
better shape. No electricity to run the water pump meant no water supply to the house, including toilets. The exception was for those who had
generators and were properly prepared for such a situation.

No electricity meant medical devices couldn't be used. Patients who needed oxygen, dialysis or other electrical-powered assistance had to try to find emergency medical care. In the first few days, hospitals were severely handicapped by the same issues citizens faced.

Frozen and refrigerated food had a 12-24 hour window to be consumed. Stores were closed and food, water and ice were not available to those who hadn't stocked up.

Citizens who thought it would all be over in a few days faced a rude awakening. Restoring the city would take weeks, something that frustrated citizens and business owners anxious to get home

By state law, the mayor is a city's emergency management director. The mayor appoints an emergency management coordinator. During Rita, in Beaumont that was Fire Chief Micky Bertrand.

Bertrand and Assistant Emergency Management Coordinator R.J. Smith, along with 30 or so firefighters had spent the night at their emergency operations center at the Downtown Beaumont Fire Station Headquarters on the second floor of 400 Walnut.

"I thought I would get a little sleep on my air mattress," Betrand said. "Silly me. I got two calls from the BBC and then a call from American Morning. They wanted to know what it looked like outside. I told them we didn't know what it looked like because it was dark."

Bertrand divided his time between the station and Edison Plaza, also known as the Entergy building, participating in unified conference calls.

Most of the firefighters were with other emergency responders, officials and elected officials at the Beaumont EOC, where restoration efforts were centralized.

As Beaumont Mayor Goodson worked with Griffith, Beaumont City Manager Kyle Hayes worked with streets and drainage, public health, solid waste, police and firefighters.

"All have an integral part after a storm. Our priorities were first clearing streets, getting water and sewer back up and functioning and of course, police were protecting neighborhoods and businesses while working 12-hour shifts," Hayes said. "The fire department was going door to door checking on residents while still providing fire protection across the city. Our parks and recreation employees were helping streets and drainage clear the streets. It's not their normal function, but they worked as a team. We had trees blocking roadways all through the city. That was a big job, and they were out there with chainsaws. All streets were open in a matter of days. You might not be able to accommodate two-way traffic, but one lane was open. Our goal was to be able to get emergency vehicles through. Our employees did an incredible job. Getting water and sewer back up took a little longer."

For law enforcement, the first priority was establishing a presence in the community to maintain order in a decidedly disorderly situation. Brit Featherston and the U.S. Attorney's office provided support.

"We were making sure we prevented looting. I know Port Arthur had a few instances, as did Beaumont. It wasn't a grave problem. There had been some burglaries in Port Arthur. We requested the Houston FBI SWAT team, and they came in and caught them. Smash-and-grab looters are on your mind. We had several cases, including breaking into a gun store in Port Arthur. We prosecuted those individuals," Featherston said.

The bad news is when a community is in peril, a lot of rats come out of the woodwork, Goodson said. The good news is law enforcement did a great job.

"We had daylight to dark curfew, which helped officers control movement about the city," Goodson said. "I was out myself and was stopped by Beaumont Police and very politely told, 'Mayor, you need to get back down to the ship.'"

Beaumont Attorney John Reaud said he believes the value of the Beaumont officers was immeasurable.

"It was one of the finest hours for the Beaumont Police Department, especially Lt. Ray Beck, who stayed behind and helped manage law enforcement in Beaumont during the days immediately before and after Rita. They were a tremendous asset to Beaumont."

Law enforcement officers, including Texas State Troopers, enforced the curfew.

Firefighters, public works, and other city employees aided utility crews in checking for broken gas lines and hot spots. Several fires that began during the storm had been left to burn themselves out. After the storm, a lack of water meant firefighters could only to do their best to contain fires like the one at the Elks Lodge on Highway 90, which burned to the ground.

Search and rescue crews went door to door checking on those who had remained in place during the storm. Firefighters and EMS crews also made the rounds, taking the injured to makeshift emergency rooms throughout the area.

As difficult as restoration was, it would have taken much longer without the support of people from outside the area who gave generously of their time, energy and money. One group came to the aid of the Southeast Texas Regional Airport, which was critical to getting planes, equipment and people to the area during restoration.

At the airport, Hal Ross's maintenance guys were contending with massive damage. Seventeen steel buildings were blown apart and scattered twisted sheet metal around the other buildings. All the glass in the tower had shattered and fallen down the stairs three levels below. Ceiling tiles swollen with rain crumbled on the floor in pools of water.

Byproducts of the emergency evacuation of 8,500 people over 30 hours filled the terminal.

"There was bio-waste everywhere – IVs and diapers and blood products," Ross said. "One pressurized hangar exploded. There was a Gulfstream jet sitting in there that was wrecked and three other planes were upside down. Philpott had just moved into another hangar and it was full of cars. What saved another building is when the door blew in and hit a row of cars, the cars held the door so the building couldn't pressurize and explode. Our airfield was full of metal, and we had no power."

Water stood on the primary runway, but at 1:45 p.m. Sunday the first helicopter landed. Later that night a Coast Guard C-130 radioed in using the intercom because the tower wasn't back up. Ross told them the lights were off, but they thought the runway was clear. Ross warned them about the standing water and added that there might be some birds nearby.

The pilot told Ross, "We're coming in."

"About 300 white egrets had congregated on the runway – and here's the plane coming in with four turbine jet engines with props. He sucked up about 200 of those egrets into that outboard port engine, but safely landed. Three days later they had the whole engine changed out. Those are brave men. They were on a mission."

The airport still had no running water, no bathrooms and no portapotties. When some resourceful soul spotted a deer stand, they cut a hole in the seat and put a five gallon bucket under it.

"That was our bathroom," Ross said.

A military flight dropped off crates of bottled water, but the airport forklift wasn't big enough to handle the pallets. Workers lugged each package off by hand.

When they secured two generators, Maintenance Supervisor Danny Nichols used one of them to power airfield lights. The others powered about 10 percent of the Jerry Ware terminal.

Jefferson County Sheriff Mitch Woods brought in some work release prisoners who started cleaning up the glass and putting in ceiling tiles. Southeast Texas Regional Airport Fire Chief Duke Youmans called his brother-in-law in Houston and asked for help.

"Within four hours, we had an 18-wheeler roll up that had a 40-ton air conditioner, a generator and a fuel tank, all self-contained, and 100 feet of 14-inch hose. We parked it behind the terminal, ran the hose in the back door, sealed it off and started blowing air in there. By about 9 Sunday night we had the place cooled down."

Airport personnel began trickling back in. At any given moment 50 to 150 Marines, Air Force and Coast Guard personnel were asking Ross, "Where can we stay?"

"They didn't bring living facilities. They did bring MREs and water, and they shared with us. That helped us for three days. We still had no showers and a 5-gallon bucket for a portapotty. It was pretty rank."

Ross, who slept on the terminal floor, said the number of people at the airport was in constant flux.

"I remember going to bed one night and during the night I heard something. About 30 guys came in from somewhere. At that point, it was find yourself a little corner and don't worry about it. You'd go to bed and there might be 20 guys and you wake up and there might be 50. I didn't know who was coming and going."

On Sunday, a tall, imposing man stepped up to Ross and said, "Hi. I'm Chris Rose. What can we do for you?"

"Who are you?" Ross asked.

"We're from the San Diego Airport."

"What are you doing here?"

"We were sent here to help you."

Nonsense, Ross thought. There is no way a group could drive to Southeast Texas from San Diego in that time. As it turned out, the group had been working for three weeks to help the New Orleans airport get back up after Hurricane Katrina.

"There were nine guys," Ross said. "I asked, 'Do you know anything about airports?'"

Today, Ross laughs about his response to their offer of help.

"Yeah," Rose answered. "We're all maintenance people, and we're cross-trained. I'm an electrician, and I can do roofing. I've got a roofer over here and a plumber. I've got a carpenter, a radio man, and a couple of laborers."

Ross checked his badge and said, "OK. Here is our airport layout plan.

Here's our charter for the airport. The tower is still closed. You've got airfield radios?"

"Yes."

"Do you know our frequencies?"

"Yes."

"Then check with the tower, get out there and check my runways. One of my biggest problems is we need to get fences up."

Ross' airport guardian angels stayed 21 days.

"Twenty-one days," Ross said, shaking his head. "And they were just phenomenal."

The nine-man crew was part of Southeast Airport Disaster Organization Group (SEADOG). The group is "an informal collection of airports who have come together to provide operational assistance to airports hit by natural disasters, such as hurricanes or floods, coordinating fast responses to specific operational needs, supplying teams of volunteer airport staff and necessary equipment needed to return an airport to operational status," according to SEADOG. The group has a Western U.S. counterpart in WESDOG.

SEADOG brought a full self-contained travel trailer equipped with tools, a cargo truck with plywood and ceiling tiles, carpet tiles and other needed supplies.

"One thing about FAA airports is we're all the same. We all have airport layout plans, our acronyms are all the same, our security and tower procedures are all the same and files are easy to access," Ross said.

Within a day or two after the SEADOGS arrived, members of the Houston Airport System arrived to help, Ross said. They worked primarily on repairing the Jerry Ware Terminal.

Four days after the storm, the county moved its EOC from Edison Plaza to the Elegante Hotel, which provided rooms for workers and a place large enough to accommodate emergency response operations. There, Griffith and emergency management coordinators continued to make calls to the State of Texas, FEMA, and other federal emergency response departments.

For days, Griffith had been taking calls from surrounding county judges who needed help but who either weren't sure how to go about it or whose requests were being ignored. The needs were many: generators, ambulances, debris removal crews, food, water, ice, search and rescue teams, and law enforcement to help patrol the outlying areas – the list went on and on.

His biggest frustration was dealing with a sluggish and unresponsive federal team. Texans came together to find answers to the struggle for recovery, Griffith said, the way Texans always have done, but they often were working in a vacuum.

"Except for our local congressional and senate leaders, Congress didn't recognize the extent of our needs," Griffith said. "The governor and the people in the state of Texas understood it, but the other folks around the nation didn't. We clearly had the attention of the entire state. Gov. Perry spent a lot of time down here with me, working very hard to help."

During one of his conversations with the governor at the EOC, Griffith told Perry that he had located a generator in Oklahoma that would run the courthouse and jail, which were in bad shape, but it would be costly. The guy who had the generator told Griffith he could drive it to Beaumont and have it on site in 8 to 10 hours.

"I told the governor, the generator is over $400,000. I need it, but the county is going to need your help. He said buy it, and put it at the courthouse. True to his word, after the storm, the governor made sure it was paid for."

Griffith found an ally and friend in Department of Homeland Security Director Steve MCraw, who now is director of the Texas Department of Public Safety. When Gov. Perry flew in to assess damages in Southeast Texas, he asked Griffith to do a flyover with him to point out the areas that had been hardest hit and had the greatest needs. McCraw took over Griffith's role as leader at the EOC so he could be confident the recovery was in the best possible hands.

Another high priority was securing the petrochemical refineries. The processes used to refine oil and other products include volatile, toxic chemicals that could cause a major environmental disaster if not handled properly. Plant managers like Lori Ryerkerk of ExxonMobil were among the first industry leaders in to inspect the properties.

Her team of 22 went first to check on their homes and then back to the plant. Ryerkerk sent them in pairs because she didn't want anyone alone. The generators in the control rooms at the plant provided air, power and a place from which to work.

In a little more than a week, Entergy had restored one feeder, and ExxonMobil was able to run their generators and return 100 megawatts of power to Entergy's grids.

"We became a primary feeder for them. Joe Domino worked with us, and we thought, if we're smart about this, we can get the entire community up," Ryerkerk said.

Refinery employees wanted to come back to work in the plant, not to be out in the community, Ryerkerk said. Griffith advised her not to bring the staff back too soon unless they could be self-sufficient and not place an additional burden on the emergency responders.

"Our chemical plant manager Dick Townsend found a cruise boat with 300 rooms out of New Orleans and brought it in, giving us instant living quarters. We rented it for $1 million a day and brought it up the river. That's how we were able to get contractors back in. Our contractors brought Moncla's Caterers in with their crew and equipment. We used local vendors to help them get their people back. We brought in a doctor twice a week from Houston. We wanted to make sure we were self-sufficient. Carl trusted that I would take care of them if I said I would."

Motiva, TOTAL, Valero and other refineries provided one of the most needed commodities after the storm – fuel. It proved challenging for ExxonMobil, which is accustomed to shipping fuel out, not bringing it in.

"We don't usually keep more than a couple hundred thousand barrels in fuel-ready tanks," Ryerkerk said. "We brought fuel in from a Russian ship. Our docks weren't set up to pump out. But we had creative people who knew everything about the refinery. By day three we were putting fuel in the refinery in order to get it out to the community. We kept no records. We distributed literally millions of gallons of fuel. As far as I know, there was never any request for payment. We considered it a donation to our community."

In a heavily unionized area like Southeast Texas, there could have been major roadblocks to a quick recovery, she said.

"Union President Mark Hidalgo said, 'Do whatever needs to be done.' We were working daylight to sundown – 16 hours – and crafts and skills didn't matter. If they could do it safely, they did. At times like this, you see what people are made of. The union easily could have slowed everything down and been completely within their rights. They stepped up and got the job done."

Although ExxonMobil opened the plant on day three, it was 20 days before they could begin making product again.

"We did a lot to help people, but so did many others. It showed what a strong community you have," said Ryerkerk, who left Beaumont in

2007 and now is Shell's vice president for manufacturing operations in Europe and Africa.

Along with fuel, the single most needed piece of equipment was generators. Without them, there was no hope for the power needed to pump fuel, operate emergency vehicles, and perform numerous other functions critical to recovery.

Robert Hobbs, supervisor and assistant U.S. Attorney, was about three to four hours out from Beaumont when his boss, Matt Orwig, called with a project. A Taiwanese charity-based organization acquired 400 generators they wanted to go to first responders.

Hobbs, who spent 20 years as a police officer and whose two brothers remain in law enforcement, didn't hesitate.

"Orwig was at one of the other offices and needed more boots on the ground. Brit Featherston had made himself indispensable at that time. My primary assignment was to receive and find an equitable way to distribute those generators. We decided to concentrate on police officers in Jefferson County. I allotted them to the Beaumont police department, Port Arthur police department, Sheriff's office and Mid-County law enforcement. When you are the possessor of 400 generators, you are the most loved – and the most hated man alive at that moment, depending on whether you are receiving one," Hobbs said.

"For equity's sake, we set up lotteries. There was no other fair way. Probably a third of the Beaumont police officers got one, a third to the Sheriff's Department and a third went to the Port Arthur Police Department. Then Lowes and Home Depot brought in window air-conditioning units. That was great because officers could get back in their homes, and then open them up so fellow officers could eat a hot meal and take a shower."

Hobbs joined in any way he could, assisting Orwig, Griffith and Featherston while watching his house mold before his eyes in the relentless heat and humidity. It was the most miserable three weeks of his life, he said.

"And just when I'm feeling most overwhelmed, being pulled from pillar to post, 12 DEA (Drug Enforcement Agency) agents showed up in my driveway with axes and chain saws. They cut 10-12 tons of trees off my house and took them to the curb. They didn't come to be officers. They came to work. They helped federal employees first, then made their way though the list and asked 'Who else needs help?' It was very emotional. Within four hours, there were multiple crews of 25 to 30 agents working

on their own time. That allowed me to focus completely on the generator project. It put me two weeks ahead so I could bring my own family
home. We couldn't live there, but I could keep it from degenerating
further."

Once the generators were squared away and office restoration was
under control, Hobbs paid it forward in a big way.

"I had access to a truck and gas so I started with our 50 employees,
most of who still were evacuated. Ninety percent of their refrigerators
and freezers were full. You know what that means – rotting food. It was
the nastiest thing. I can't tell you how many times I puked on Beaumont
streets. I got them to the curb in black garbage bags. After two days in
the sun, the city required us to take them to a disposal site. The bags
would burst all over my shoes and in my truck," he laughed. "I don't
know that I'd do that again."

Hobbs would call up those he knew and ask, "Do you have a key hid-
den outside so I can get in?"

"No," they said. "Break a window."

"For a man who spent his entire career as a police officer and pros-
ecutor, it was surreal," Hobbs said. I'm standing there with a hammer
shattering glass and breaking into homes."

Hobbs, who has worked with and supervised public servants throughout his career, understands the personality and skills needed to be an
effective leader. He was proud of what he saw from those in charge after
the storm.

"Brit is an adrenalin junkie. He loves a crisis. I think that comes from
his years as a police officer. And from what I saw, Carl Griffith, Pat
Grimes and the Beaumont Fire Department were true leaders. They
were able to focus on one thing in the midst of chaos to get it to a conclusion. The sheer volume of crises can overwhelm to the point you're
making no progress on any of them. They chose the hottest fires, put
them out and then moved on to the next. There were so many people
willing to work but they needed direction," Hobbs said. "I was a frequent
presence in the command post, and I noticed that fire officials had an
insight into problems I wouldn't have anticipated. They saw things that
others did not. Grimes was worth his weight in gold. He was cool, calm
and collected. He and Brit were together and would see solutions to
problems."

Griffith's approach to leadership has been forged through years of
experience.

"I thought Hurricane Rita was the high point in a positive administration. Carl is at his best when it's fast moving and he's making constant decisions," Hobbs said.

"Everybody has an opinion on what they think a leader is," Griffith said. "Clearly, for me, it's prioritizing the issues. What are the things that put us in harm's way and what can we do to immediately mitigate those? Who can best meet that need? You don't necessarily know that, so you ask questions and then listen to the feedback from the people who are there. The person whose solution sounds the most logical to be able to make that thing happen at any given time – that's the person you assign the task to. You expect it to be done and you hold them accountable if they don't get it done, just as you recognize them if they do."

Griffith, who began his career as a street cop, then worked in the jail system, has a master's degree in counseling that helps him analyze situations and make appropriate determinations. But success depends on having experienced people around you to tackle problems and find potential solutions, he said. A good leader seeks them out.

"I was incredibly impressed with the team at the EOC. Of course I had friends who were firefighters and fire chiefs. But I had never been in a situation quite like this where I had those particular invaluable resources at my side when I made decisions that impacted the entire community. I knew the law enforcement side of it, but the part I never really thought about is how firefighters know the entire community and have keys to access its resources. They also knew how to leverage and get those assets."

Along with firefighters helping run the EOC were police officers running the fuel system, along with some local folks in the fuel distribution business, which was critical.

"We also had a lieutenant with the Highway Patrol, a senior resident agent in charge from the FBI in Houston, and five of his agents. Those people had valuable information about assets available through the state and nation," Griffith said. "Firefighters were calling and searching all over the country and coming to me every minute with answers: here's what we can do. They came up with solutions to the largest issues we faced and we vetted them out. I was incredibly impressed with their ingenuity."

Featherston, who watched Griffith handle a constant series of crises day after day, said he was struck by the sense of unity projected by those working toward restoration under conditions none of them had ever before experienced.

"When it came to critical hurricane issues, Carl never missed forgot that he was speaking for the entire region," Featherston said. "We were constantly receiving requests from Bevil Oaks or Hamshire and other small towns needing help. We forwarded those through the state EOC to be deployed through FEMA. The process through the state just wasn't working fast enough, and we would get tired of waiting. When he was arguing for resources, there were pretty heated conversations. Carl was a big part of why the response to Rita was as successful as it was. He did not accept no for an answer."

Across Southeast Texas, while emergency management coordinators worked to evaluate the area's infrastructure and make plans for restoring local governments and services, the medical community had its own set of challenges.

Family Practice Physician James Larry Holly had ridden out the storm at Edison Plaza at the suggestion of Griffith and first responders who thought it would be a good idea to have a doctor available for any emergencies. Holly, who volunteered to help with the post-storm medical response, thought it would be one of the safest places to be during the hurricane.

"I'm not afraid of dying, but I don't want to die stupidly. To die for a noble cause, to save a child's life, for instance, is something most of us would do. But to die for a stupid reason? No."

Early Saturday morning, when the winds dropped some, two Beaumont firefighters drove Holly to Memorial Hermann Baptist Hospital, which had evacuated patients and kept a skeleton staff. Holly planned to set up an emergency center there for ambulatory care. That didn't prove feasible.

"They weren't able to handle emergencies because their water was polluted. The reality is when a hospital does not have potable water, they are out of business. Every machine they've got is dependent on water and every patient safety feature is dependent on safe and secure water supply. It shows you how vulnerable we are with the absence of usable water."

On Sunday, without patients to see, Holly quickly grew restless.

"To maintain sanity, I started cleaning. I cleaned all the neighborhood yards. On Monday I had a chain saw and was down on my knees cutting a limb off my neighbor's fence. A guy drove by and said 'Do you live here?'

"No."

"Why are you cleaning the yard?"

"I said, they are my neighbors, and they are gone. I've got my yard cleaned up, and it seems the decent thing to do," Holly said. "There was a lot of that going on. I am still close to people six years later in my neighborhood I'd never met before Rita. Human beings need each other. We cannot live in isolation. It's not the way we prosper. People congregated and reached out to one another."

By Sunday, Memorial Hermann Baptist Hospital in Beaumont had reopened its emergency room and was seeing patients, with the help of a DMAT team from Massachusetts, said Donna Biscamp, an R.N. in the emergency department.

"A large number of staff members and physicians stayed at the hospital during the storm, so they were ready to go when the storm was over," Biscamp said. "We were able to treat the emergency portion of the patient's need and then transfer them to other hospitals that were operational. By Sunday evening, the DMAT team had come in and assisted us in caring for patients. They brought in ambulance services and everything we needed. They could actually do transfers faster than we could," Biscamp said.

The DMAT team left after two weeks once the hospital was fully operational.

Christus St. Elizabeth Hospital furnished a large generator at Southeast Texas Medical Associates on Calder, where Holly and his partners practice, allowing them to operate their clinic.

In Port Arthur, Police Chief Mark Blanton was concerned about being able to rapidly respond to medical emergencies, whether among his department or the general public. He knew from experience that emergencies can – and will – happen.

While assisting one of his officers when a Katrina evacuee fired a shot at him, Blanton was bitten by a spider. The bite became infected and he had to have surgery. The day after he was released from the hospital, he began evacuating his city for Rita.

After Rita, the City of Port Arthur set up an emergency room at the Holiday Inn, where people showed up who had been bitten by dogs, injured during the storm or while cleaning up afterward, or with general health issues.

Emergency responders faced injuries as well, such as gasoline, fuel or other chemicals in their eyes, heat exhaustion, cuts and abrasions and even appendicitis.

Blanton was concerned because his city, as well as Nederland, Port Neches and Groves, had no ambulances the first couple of days to respond to emergencies. He called Judge Griffith at Ford Park and asked for ambulances. Griffith thought centralizing dispatch at the park was the best way to see that ambulances went where they were needed. Blanton didn't agree.

"I said, 'Carl, that's too long a response time. The response from Ford Park to Port Arthur is 30 minutes at least, especially with debris on the road from the hurricane.' If someone got electrocuted, by the time an ambulance left Ford Park and came all the way to Port Arthur, somebody would be dead. We kind of got into an argument, and I ended up talking with State Representative Joe Deshotel. He and Carl worked something out and the next thing I knew, I had ambulances from Ford Park."

Blanton set up a dispatch office at the Stonegate Fire Station and notified Mid-County cities that ambulances were available for them.

Forward-thinking Jefferson County Health Department Director Dr. Cecil Walkes had secured generators before Rita, and moved all medications and vaccines into temperature-controlled storage so they would be stable and useable, even with a power outage. He made sure that all first responders who would come in contact with contaminated water and debris after the storm were adequately protected by initiating a vaccination campaign.

Confident that the clinic could be brought back up quickly, Walkes had joined other city and county staffers on the Cape Vincent on Friday to be immediately available for any emergency care.

As soon as the storm passed and emergency responders began their work, Walkes opened the pharmacy, filling prescriptions for anyone who needed them. Because his pharmacist had evacuated with family, Walkes was the only one with the necessary credentials. Three county nurses who had stayed during the storm helped him provide medical care in the 10 days before all his nurses returned.

Walkes, who slept on the Cape Vincent for a month, accompanied law enforcement on a windshield survey, providing tetanus and hepatitis A and B vaccinations to first responders in Nederland, Groves and Port Neches. He went inside refineries that were keeping workers through the storm, vaccinating them as well. As workers began pouring in from outside the area, he did the same for them.

Next on the list was setting up medical clinics in each city. Some were in churches, other in fire stations.

Walkes and his staff kept long hours; his nurses worked until after midnight when Entergy and Entex utility crews arrived late in the evening and needed their vaccinations. They went inside refineries and anywhere else work crews needed protection.

Most of the medical care at the clinics was for minor cuts, bruises and rashes, as well as colds and chest problems.

"We had all the drugs and vaccines we needed here and kept the pharmacy going. We did run out of vaccines, and we made a trip down to Baytown to pick some up. Our pharmacist called me from East Texas to say there were 400-500 people without medical attention. She was looking to me to take care of those people up there," he said, laughing and shaking his head. "So I was just about to send some medical help to her from Austin when somehow Austin got in touch with them and sent a team."

Walkes was especially concerned about the elderly, who became most at risk during the evacuation. Usually, nursing homes have arrangements to transport their patients to another nursing home out of the storm's path, whether by ambulance or buses. With the elderly, any change in routine can exacerbate existing medical conditions. Without a doubt, the trauma of the evacuation hastened deaths.

"With elderly people, even moving from their home to the hospital can make them become disoriented and confused- and that is a friendly place, compared with another state where they don't know anyone. I could see that putting them on a plane and sending them from here to Atlanta – where many people were sent – could escalate their problems. It's a hostile environment, and it's very difficult. They deteriorate quickly. You have the family going one place, and the nursing home patients going somewhere else. You can't bring the two together. In that kind of situation you are going to have these problems. I don't know how you could be able to correct it unless you evacuated the patient with his or her relatives. It's very difficult to have a one-on-one situation where family takes the person out of the nursing home to Dallas or wherever. That's the only way I can see that there would be some familiarity, and they may prevent these types of things."

A lack of centralized and easily accessibly medical records presented another challenge. Few patients had medical records with them, hampering efforts by medical providers. With the elderly, the patient often can't provide that information.

Compounding the problem was the effort to locate patients. The limited time to get medical special needs out on planes meant no one knew where the patients were going. Once they arrived, HIPPA laws that protect a patient's privacy prevented the medical providers from being able even to confirm that they did, indeed, have a particular patient.

Now, many hospitals and medical providers in Jefferson County are moving toward computerized records so they will be immediately available in any location.

Prior to the storm, as part of the Jefferson County EOC team at the Marine Safety Unit in Port Arthur, Captain Pat Grimes worked with other regional team members to build lists of home health patients, hospice patients, and other special needs patients who did not have transportation to evacuate.

The team called everyone on the list prior to sending transportation to take them out of harm's way. If the patient didn't answer, firefighters would be sent to check on them and make sure they had a way out.

The team received numerous faxes and phone calls from people all across the region needing transportation assistance. If the evacuee was not from Jefferson County, the call was forwarded to the correct jurisdiction for processing.

"It was very important no evacuee be left behind," Grimes said.

Evacuation required all the resourcefulness and ingenuity the team could muster.

All available resources were utilized to transport the evacuees.

"We picked them up with anything we could do. We had two school buses from Nederland ISD that we took to the Stiles (prison) unit and took the seats out. We used those to transport bed bound patients to the airport. As the airlift intensified, we used fire department chief cars and rescue vehicles with the back seats removed as another resource."

After the storm, Firefighter Clem Stinebrickner suggested that he use his database expertise to post their master list to make it accessible to everyone in the EOC.

Grimes and Stinebrickner used the bus and air manifests created during the Rita evacuation to support home inspections. Firefighters would check to see if the home had water, electricity, gas and if it was in good enough condition for the evacuee to come home. The storm had left the area with any motel, hotel or other available housing.

The results of those home checks were entered into the database and forwarded to shelters so evacuees would know the condition of their homes before they committed to returning.

"All the men and women at the EOC worked extremely hard to get our citizens back," Grimes said. "We had never done anything like this and everyone came together to work it out. To me, this was typical of the whole Rita EOC experience. As situations arose, everyone worked hard to find a solution and got the job done."

Following Rita, Grimes and Stinebrickner worked together to develop the Sabine Neches Chiefs Association special needs database, which also includes contact information for emergency response teams, emergency managers, media, elected officials, and state and national resources.

The database became an invaluable source of information emergency workers now use to locate and evacuate the 6,000 to 7,000 special needs folks in Southeast Texas, utilizing the Area Agency on Ageing 2-1-1 registry system. Other additions included State-issued identification wrist bands for each person and pet. The wrist bands include name, bus assignments and shelter locations.

After Rita, Pat Grimes, who now is Assistant Emergency Management Coordinator, conducted two full-scale drills that were critical to ensure success in future evacuations. One drill was at the Beaumont Civic Center, the medical special needs evacuation site. The other drill was at Beaumont West Brook High School, the site for general population evacuation. The drill used all the components that would be used in an actual evacuation. They issued students a s evacuees, registering them, scanning them in using bar code scanners, placed a wrist band on them and entered them into a manifest, loaded them on a bus. After driving the students around, they were registered at their destination "shelter."

It went off without a hitch, Grimes said, and the lesson learned from the drills became invaluable later during the evacuations of Hurricanes Gustav and Ike in 2008.

St. Elizabeth Hospital now has an up-to-the-hour computerized medical record system that will keep patients and their records together wherever they are.

"We came up with a packet that has medical records that go around their neck. They contain all the medical information, who to contact, what hospital we talked to about taking them when they evacuate, and anything else that is needed. These are all pre-printed and we have them ready whenever we need them. We shared the plan with all the other hospitals in our Christus system because you can use them for a fire or any other kind of disaster."

The type of problem-solving the fire department showed was echoed throughout the department, which furnished the largest contingent during the city's emergency operations.

"Our entire department rose to the task. They put their heart and soul into trying to make it right for people. Every single person who worked here went beyond the job description, even working to put blue tarps on houses," said Anne Huff, now chief of the department. "Beaumont fire personnel came together to do what needed to be done, not just for our community, but for the surrounding area, too. Nobody griped or complained. We did what we had to do to help people. That's what our mission is."

During daily briefings, Mayor Guy Goodson listened to reports of the condition of the city. It wasn't long before he found himself defending one of the most difficult decisions he had to make and enforce – keeping the evacuation order in place for three weeks. The mayor did allow citizens to come back in, check on their homes and secure them, for one day only, from 8 a.m. to 5 p.m. While some stayed, others quickly realized Southeast Texas was not the safest place to be if they had another option.

While some citizens and business owners anxious to come home were angry about the extended evacuation, others had no desire to return to a city in chaos. A city with downed electrical lines, trees across the road, dangerous debris everywhere, and no water, sewer, food sources and limited medical care was not the place to be without a really good reason.

Entergy leaders, who had given their input, were grateful.

"Not having traffic for the first week was very helpful. Having the city closed allowed us to get a lot of work done. It's very difficult to move around the city streets with line trucks and crews blocking traffic. Some people wanted to just look. Some were trying to find stores that were open," Vernon Pierce said.

Deciding when to lift the evacuation created some tense moments between Goodson and Griffith, both of whom felt the responsibility to make the best decision they could.

"We did argue amongst ourselves but it was good dialogue," Griffith said. "Ultimately Guy and I got into an argument over how long we should keep citizens out. He wanted me to keep the mandatory evacuation on Jefferson County, which I didn't want to do."

Griffith, who owns a ranch in rural western Jefferson County, knew what being away from their land would do to farmers and ranchers with livestock needing care.

"I explained to him that ranchers all over the county had their own water wells, windmills, and generators, and they had to take care of their stock or they would die. He was dealing with a different animal because he had a city where the sewer system was shut down, and they didn't have water. People in the country are on septic system, and they don't have that issue – the fear of disease because of a lack of fresh water and toilets.

"I had people calling me saying I've got cattle or I've got chicken or other animals at my ranch. I've got to go back in and take care of them or they're going to die. I wasn't going to see those animals suffer and die in a pen. Mayors make the decisions on the city. I made the decision about the unincorporated area."

Griffith heard that Goodson was unhappy about his decision to lift the order on the unincorporated areas of the county. He found Goodson at a checkpoint on Interstate 10 and talked with him about the decision.

"We had a heated discussion about it. It didn't mean we weren't friends; we just had a difference of opinion. His focus was on the city and what he felt was best for the citizens of Beaumont with the infrastructure the way it was. I knew what it was like living in an un-incorporated area."

When Goodson lifted the evacuation order, citizens came home to begin the long, stressful, work of rebuilding their homes and lives.

Chapter Nine

Beginning Recovery

Experiencing the extreme stress of a natural disaster
such as Hurricane Rita tends to heighten the emotions. While it can
make for some testy moments during the decision-making process,
struggling through the long, painful recovery can stay with those carrying the responsibility for others.

The fear of what might happen if they didn't evacuate drove people
to join the historic evacuation prior to Rita's landfall, but the anxiety remained after the storm slowly moved north, dumping rain and spawning
tornadoes along the way.

Those who waited out the storm at home had awakened – if they
slept at all – to discover they had no electricity, no sewer service and no
potable water. Only the ones with enough foresight to plan for such
things – as they had been told to time and time again – had adequate
food and water. Those able to buy generators were in better shape, but
still had to contend with the loss of basic services.

As it had before the storm, it fell to the first responders to take care
of their cities. They had done everything they knew to do within the
time they had to prepare. They moved to a place of safety, watched and
listened to the storm rage, then began the hard work of recovery.

First on the list was assessing damage so they could set priorities for cleanup and restoration of city, county and state governments.

When Port Neches Mayor Glenn Johnson and his team got back into Port Neches after the storm, they began following pre-determined priorities.

"First, police have to secure the city right off the bat. Our police chief at the time was Gene Marsh. I told Gene, this is my philosophy on looting in the city of Port Neches, there will be none. Period. That's all I had to tell him," Johnson said.

"It's the principle of the thing. People have to get out of town during bad times. If someone wants to take advantage of that, I've got zero sympathy. I don't care what the ACLU or anyone else says. I really don't. A week after the storm, three individuals broke into a store on the corner of Nederland Avenue and Magnolia and by the time they got down the street, our police already had them in custody. We arrested them and took them to jail."

While law enforcement secured the city, the public works department assessed broken water and sewer lines and other damaged city infrastructure. The fire department surveyed the city for gas leaks and hazardous conditions, including non-operational fire hydrants. All departments provided assessment reports to the mayor.

In Port Neches, the public works director reported that the water plant control center was down. A suspected tornado had ripped it apart and plunged the control center into a tank of water.

"At the time, the assessment was it would be several weeks before we could get drinkable water in the city. But to show you the type of employees we have here in the city – that was on Saturday. Tuesday they had built a makeshift emergency control center and were operating the water treatment plant. So we actually had water – not potable water, because it was on a generator and you have to have electricity to it. There was water for sewer and for showers and stuff like that," Johnson said.

"When we came back in Saturday my command center was already set up. The way it works is the city manager (Andre Weimer) goes to the command center, and then all the others go out and make assessments, then come in and make reports to me. We had generators at all the key building – city hall, fire department and police department. The fuel tanks at public works were full, and we were stocked. "

Before long, the city began running low on fuel. When a contractor hired to refuel the tanks couldn't get through the roadblocks, TOTAL refinery came to the rescue, supplying the needed fuel.

When Steve Curran returned to Port Neches, he noticed that his small city's team was not coordinating efforts. Public works, police and fire departments all were operating independently, which limited communication and created duplications of efforts. He called a meeting with the mayor and key leaders to sketch out exactly how they would operate during the recovery.

The city set up its emergency operations center in the police department courtroom, and the fire station became the kitchen. Once they set the schedule, they stuck to it, mitigating as they went along, Curran said.

In the midst of the chaos, operating as one team is critical. The hardest part is choosing the key leaders, he said, because the incident command system calls for them to remain in the operations center to direct efforts. That's hard for first responders who are used to being in the middle of the action, making things happen.

"You no longer get to go out and play. It's too easy to go out in the field. That's the fun part. You have to stay in the operations and deal with emergency management issues and statutes and legal issues and that kind of thing. You have to corral your leaders. Once we did that, we were good to go."

While Curran was helping direct emergency response, he relied heavily on his Assistant Chief, Shawn Gearinger, to conduct search and rescue from house to house, shutting off gas leaks and helping clear debris from the streets to make them passable. The public works department was focused on getting the water plant back up and running.

On the plus side, the emergency generators the city had installed in the fire station, police station and city hall all functioned as they should. Although the roofs leaked, the facilities were intact. The downed water plant was a priority.

"The electronics of the plant fell into the pit of water. There is a line, a valve between the city of Nederland and Port Neches that would allow us to draw Nederland water into Port Neches. We thought we were going to have to do that, but we didn't. They shook it out, cleaned it up, got it working again and scabbed together a place and reset it. It was pretty awesome," Curran said.

With the water system down and fires breaking out in homes because of storm damage and broken gas lines, the city called for tenders, which are tanker trucks filled with water. After fighting with the state, Curran said, a California group of the U.S. Forest Service came in to help.

The fire department needed to transport supplies from place to place but didn't have enough equipment. They "borrowed" a truck from Philpott Ford, which they purchased after Rita and still use today.

After securing the safety of the citizens, many of their efforts went toward taking care of those who were taking care of the city.

"We scavenged refrigerated trucks and went down to the ice plant and got their truck. We commandeered whatever we needed to make things work. We robbed the food from the school district's freezers and met with them. They told us, 'We'll feed you.' We had DPS officers here and state fire marshals. Many of them were sent in by the state with nothing. That was one of our biggest complaints. We're trying to take care of ourselves and you're bumming off us. Well, we did it. We took care of all our people," Curran said.

Although Mark Blanton wasn't officially named chief of police in Port Arthur until two months after Rita, he had been acting chief for a number of months while the chief was seriously ill.

Blanton, an intense leader who seldom minces words, still feels today the frustrations he encountered during Rita while directing efforts to help secure the second largest city in Jefferson County.

The city's emergency plan called for establishing an emergency operations center at the Holiday Inn. Blanton's reasoning was its location next to the Medical Center of Southeast Texas and large parking lots at the nearby shopping center that could become a storage and staging center for equipment.

Having the Holiday Inn as an operations center was invaluable to restoring and maintaining order, said John Owens.

"We established a city government at the Holiday Inn including the operations center, following the Incident Command System (ICS) structure. The police department established a temporary holding facility for any people who needed to be incarcerated before we were able to take them to Jefferson County Jail, which they opened later in downtown Beaumont. At our operations facility, we had our chief elected officials, which included councilmen and all our department heads."

Owens and Blanton believe one of the best decisions the city could have made was signing a contract with a disaster response company with a local office. To their knowledge, no other city in the region had one.

"It was a godsend. After Rita, it was amazing all the cities, especially here locally, that got them," Blanton said.

"We had already developed a push package of critical components we would need. We knew we were probably going to lose our electricity. Utilities would be out. The company pre-staged generators big enough to run the fire stations, other critical facilities, and the Holiday Inn, with which they had an emergency contract agreement," Owens added. "I actually wrote seizure orders for the mayor. I told him the next morning, by the way, you seized a hotel last night through your emergency powers. He said, 'I can do that?' I said, yes, you can right now. We needed it for housing for the DPS, Houston Police Department and other people coming to help. We were able to seize three or four hotels around the Holiday Inn and hook the generators up in them so they were self-sufficient, too."

The hotel was on board 100 percent, Owens said, because they then had electricity and the ability to work on their own issues.

"Within 72 hours we had a huge 40-foot trailer and two-meg generator. You would have thought Entergy had hooked up the Holiday Inn. They had air conditioning, a kitchen, even a lighted pool. Everything worked. We were working emergency 12-hour shifts and were the envy of the whole county. All our cops and firemen and public works people were able to eat a hot meal and go to bed in an air-conditioned room. The housekeeping staff washed all our clothes. Esther Benoit from Esther's Seafood Restaurant had lost her business and had all kinds of seafood that was going to ruin. She came down and we said, 'Do you want a room, Esther?' She became our chef. Other than the stress of having to deal with it, it was unbelievable," Blanton said.

As difficult as recovery would be those first critical days, it would have been much worse without the help of business and industry.

"We pretty much became self-sufficient. We ran out of toiletries and other supplies at one point. I had an officer stationed at Wal-Mart. We would go get items, write the bar code and quantity of the items we took so the city could later reimburse them, which they did. Both Wal-Mart and HEB were two of the best private industries in how they handled our community. They brought in canteens and portable pharmacies so the citizens could get their prescription medicines," Blanton said.

"Our industry locally was instrumental in assuring that we had plenty of fuel," Owens noted. "They didn't keep a ticket or a log. Tom Purvis had sat in our EOC with us during the storm and after, Motiva came to us and said, 'We know you need diesel for your fire truck and public works and police cars need fuel. Come get it, or we will come to you.' Motiva, Valero and TOTAL supplied us with fuel. When we had generators delivered, they would send a fleet of electricians from TOTAL and would work 24-7 until all the generators were hooked up. They were awesome."

While South County officials were doing everything they could on their own, Owens and Blanton were fighting the bureaucracy for state aid.

"The correct way of requesting assistance is you go through the county judge, then the state. Judge Griffith said, 'You don't have to call me. You guys know what you are doing. Just go straight to the state. So I called the state operations center and said, we need some fuel assets, ice and water for PODS. They said, 'Well, we hear you, but you need to fax that information in.' I thought they were playing with me. I said, you know we don't have electricity. I can't fax anything. That's why I'm calling you," Owens said.

When he realized the person on the other end of the line was serious, he tried diplomacy.

"I said, look, please understand what we're dealing with here. She said, 'Sir, we understand but we can't approve your request unless it's in writing.' I got pretty vulgar and said several things I shouldn't."

Owens, whose frustration was rising, sensed someone standing nearby. He turned to find a well-dressed woman watching him.

"I turned and said, what the hell do you want? She grinned and said, 'Sir?'

"I said, I'm very busy, I'm not in the mood and if you are from the press, I don't have time. Please get out of my way. While still on the phone, I turned around and she said, 'Let me introduce myself.' I said a few other choice words. She hands me a card and it's Sheila Jackson Lee, the U.S. Congresswoman from Houston. I read the card and thought to myself, Uh, oh! I said, 'Ma'am I'm very sorry.' She put her arm around me and said, 'Honey, you don't have to apologize to me. You're going through so much. Bless your heart. What do you need?'

"How much time do you have?" he asked her.

Lee asked Owens who he was talking with on the phone. He told her, the State of Texas. She asked Owens, "Do you mind if I ask a few questions?"

"I said, no, ma'am, not at all. I handed her my phone and wow! She never cursed, but I could tell it was, 'Yes ma'am and 'No ma'am' on the other end. I know she doesn't even represent this area, but it meant a lot to us locally. I had an immediate call from Disaster District Office in Beaumont and they said, 'What the hell is going on?' I said, we've got some total idiots answering the phone in Austin. Y'all need to get them off their asses and make them realize we don't have time for their nonsense. That evening, I get a call from the governor's office. He said, I'm sorry about that, somebody wasn't using their head. We're going to rectify that problem."

Owens received calls from Frank Cantu of the Texas Governor's Division of Emergency Management, as well as calls from the late Jack Colley, the much-respected head of Texas' emergency management agency.

"I've got to tell you, I have the utmost respect for the state now. They learned so much from mistakes with Rita," Owens said. "It was like night and day with Hurricanes Gustav and Ike. They stepped up to the plate and provided us with a turnkey, smooth operation."

Owens said the city also was grateful for the support of Ted Poe of the Texas Second Congressional District, who fought hard to bring attention to Southeast Texas, as well as State Representative Joe Deshotel, whom he said spent countless hours helping.

"He would stay up all night with us," Owens said.

Once the storm had passed, among Deshotel's first thoughts were concerns for the poor who, unable or unwilling to evacuate, were stuck in cities that had essentially shut down.

Deshotel represents 130,000 people in parts of Beaumont, Port Arthur, Orange and Bridge City. Almost two-thirds of families with children in his district live below the poverty line. Fewer than a quarter of households have income of $50,000 or more, and 20 percent of them live on less than $20,000 a year.

Deshotel estimates that close to a third of his citizens did not evacuate. Evacuating takes money. Those who had enough gas to get to a relative's house, or enough money for a hotel were far likelier to leave. Even those who might want to take advantage of bus rides to shelters had to have a way to get to the buses and have at least some food, water and supplies for the trip. Once there, they were dependent on volunteers and organizations to provide everything. If they couldn't manage that, or didn't have enough medication, it seemed safer to stay put.

What they didn't count on was weeks in horrendous heat without electricity, sewer capability or drinking water. The air temperature at times was 100 degrees or higher, with unbearable humidity and hordes of mosquitoes, making sitting outside even more miserable. Those with medical issues were in critical need of water and food.

Deshotel also was worried about how long they would have to wait for supplies.

"Katrina was fresh in everyone's mind. We had been able to see people stranded for days with no food or water. We all watched it on TV, so there wasn't any great expectation there would be food drops from the federal government."

After the storm, Deshotel put in a call to HEB's corporate office. Within two days, the Texas-based grocery chain brought in truckloads of free ice, supplies and cookers from San Antonio. They were among the first, he said, and made no restrictions about where the food and ice would be distributed.

"They didn't tie it to HEB locations. They dropped it wherever we needed it," an appreciative Deshotel said. Within another day or two, the National Guard was delivering and distributing supplies.

Although Deshotel lives in Beaumont, he decided to spend his time at the EOC in Port Arthur, where he felt he would be most needed.

"It looked like North County – the Beaumont area – had a lot more resources and manpower available at the Entergy building than they did down in South County. They had larger fire departments and police forces in Beaumont. I spent most of my time working with the manager, mayor, police and fire departments in Port Arthur. They didn't have as much help."

Port Arthur police canvassed neighborhoods to locate residents and assess needs. When supply trucks arrived, Deshotel's son, W. Joe Deshotel, Jr. and his legislative aide, Christian Manuel, distributed ice and MREs. Deshotel called the Department of Health and Human Services in Austin to arrange for emergency food stamps. It took three to four days, in part because state workers had evacuated and no one was available to handle the applications. Closed grocery stores provided another complication, effectively shutting off access to food.

When stamps did become available, Deshotel's office issued press releases to any functioning media on where and how hungry and broke citizens could apply and pick them up.

Deshotel worked with DPS emergency chief Jack Colley to get the Texas National Guard to man PODS set up in Port Arthur. They chose places they knew people without transportation normally would congregate.

"We felt we were on our own. We needed to do it ourselves or it wouldn't get done – and we weren't going to sit around waiting on the government," he said. "When they did show up it was chaos. Ford Park had tons of supplies we needed to get out to people, but the bureaucracy was such that it sat there for days. It got to the point that it was basically taken away from them almost by force to get distributed to people who needed it. It was ridiculous the paperwork they wanted. It didn't make any sense to us."

As a state representative, Deshotel works for the government of Texas, but he had few kind words for the bureaucratic process national government employees were required to follow at the time.

"It was frustrating. The federal government people had manuals, and they had to look at them to see how to go from point "A" to "B" to "C" and then "D." They can't get to "D" without going through all the steps. It was like; I have to do this before I can do this. It was like zombies."

In Beaumont, Jefferson County Commissioner Bo Alfred was having the same anxious thoughts about the 80,000 citizens of Precinct 4. Making decisions during an event with which you have no experience can be a hit-and-miss proposition. Alfred figures he got at least three things right.

Few people outside his family and staff know that for six months, Alfred spent every night sleeping in his precinct's service center on Lafin Road. Rita's winds heavily damaged the roof and rainwater threatened to destroy everything inside. Alfred and his staff constructed a makeshift water collection system using tarpaulin and ropes. The tarps caught and held water, which dripped into strategically placed trash cans.

"We knew that after a certain time, the containers would be full, so I would set an alarm clock and we'd get up and empty them out and then get a little more rest," Alfred said. "We did that until we were able to put a roof back on."

The commissioner also put to use the one piece of equipment he most needed, a generator that was going to be sold as salvage after the county closed the juvenile facility in downtown Beaumont a couple of years before Rita.

Spotting the piece of equipment, Alfred had asked, "What's that?"

"An old generator."

"What are you going to do with it?"

"Get rid of it."

Alfred called his mechanic and asked if he thought they might use the generator. Sure, the mechanic said.

"That generator helped us through Rita. It was the reason why staff could get in. It allowed others from the county to house there with us," Alfred said. Among those who used the precinct shelter were staff members of the Department of Health and Welfare and the U.S. Attorney's office.

Alfred had learned the hard way that the type of roof his service center building had would be no match for a storm like Rita. In replacing it, he decided to go a different route, choosing an engineered-grade roof, knowing that it would take six months from start to finish.

"My grandmother raised me, and I come from humble means. She taught me that when you make a commitment, you get it done. I made that commitment. It was one of the blessings my staff received during Hurricane Ike in 2008 because that roof and that old generator enabled my staff, two constables' deputy precincts and health and welfare staff needed after Ike to stay in the service center."

Alfred and his team had secured 14 dump trucks, a couple of gradealls and other equipment on the ship at the Port of Beaumont. He used the equipment to clear trees and debris from the rural roadways so workers could get in to repair electrical lines.

The service center was well-stocked with fuel and provided gas for some emergency workers, including the U.S. Attorney's office, U.S. Marshal Service and law enforcement.

Alfred sent workers to Ford Park to pick up ice and water for citizens who hadn't evacuated or stored supplies.

"There was no electricity, and it was unbearably hot. There were some old-timers who wouldn't leave. You had people sitting on their porches all over the precinct. We didn't just stop at our precinct. We went anywhere we could help people. You have to get out of your comfort zone. A lot of those guys were staying inside. I was out on the streets where the people were. You see the need and know what you have to do. And you do it. To me, that's what it's all about. If you are a true public servant, you have to help people. If you need to, you go without to make sure that old lady and her grandsons on the porch have ice and water. That's the commitment I had to make."

The visits had a dual purpose. Alfred's team tried to reason with the residents and get them to agree to go to Ford Park to be transported to San Antonio until it was safe to come back into town.

"It was dangerous here. There were wires everywhere, trees down, utilities down. At that point our infrastructure hadn't had a hit like that in so long it showed the weaknesses we had. "

Alfred is a team builder, the type of man who believes in leading by example. While he freely offers praise to those who rise to the considerable challenges of a disaster, he also believes in calling to task those who aren't as visible.

"I'm going to say this: I believe that I have obligations to the citizens I serve to be here and to get their county up and going as soon as possible. I could not do that trying to cut my way back in. It is proven that when you are here you can work your way out and around things because you know what's there. The citizens pay us to be here. For example, it was unbearable for workers and prisoners at the county jail. Sheriff Woods was right there in the middle of it with them. The general population doesn't know about many of the things that happened. Insiders know. And they now know who will be there to cover your back. I'll put it like that."

Chapter Ten

Sabine Pass

Kristi Heid wasn't sure what she'd find when she re-
turned to her home at Sabine Pass, a tiny community on the Gulf
of Mexico at the southern tip of Jefferson County. Although she was
confident she had done the best she could to meet her responsibility to
protect her community, when Hurricane Rita finally hit, Sabine Pass was
near the eye.

The community is so small that students from 3-years-old to 12th
grade attend classes in its one school. Virtually each one of the 250
students knew Mrs. Heid, the new principal who had been on the job for
only six weeks when Rita struck.

Fortunately for the people of Sabine Pass, Heid knows the community as few do. She has lived there since she was 4, and her family has
evacuated from hurricanes numerous times. Like her, the most seasoned
residents know when to stay, she said, and when to leave. That wisdom
can mean the difference between life and death.

Heid's superintendent at the time was new to the area. When the
storm took aim at Sabine Pass, he boarded up his home and took his
family to safety. That left Heid – in her first job as a principal – in control.
Heid didn't flinch. The decisive leader who isn't afraid to make a decision

called in the school's business and technology managers to decide how to proceed with guarding the school as best they could. They secured the servers, data and other business records, then took them to what locals call the "front ridge." Although the front ridge is only four miles from the beach, it sits on a higher elevation than the school, which is 10 miles from the ocean.

Heid remembered that when she was a child, families would bring their mowers, tractors and boats and put them on her dad's 12 acres on the ridge for safekeeping during a storm.

"So I did what I needed to do," Heid said. "I took all my buses and all our stuff out there, and it was all fine."

Heid and her family left for Jasper Thursday afternoon, where they rode out the storm. When the storm's northward push took it over Jasper, the city lost electricity. Heid fretted about the school, her home and those of others as she tried without success to get much information about how Sabine Pass fared. She had to rely on word-of-mouth, and the word wasn't good.

"We were hearing it was a direct hit on Sabine Pass, and it was bad," she said.

Heid was forced to evacuate further north to Marshall. She spent one night there, most of it on the phone trying to find lodging near Sabine Pass, determined to get as close to home as possible. She finally secured rooms in Kemah. The next morning she, her husband, and son left for what would be their home for three weeks. She slept in the hotel, but spent every waking hour driving back to Sabine Pass and setting up and managing relief operations for her community.

Because the mandatory evacuation wouldn't be lifted for weeks, Heid had to find a way to get past the roadblocks. She thought her school credentials would do the trick. They did get her through two, but at the last roadblock she had to cross on Highway 73 into Port Arthur, a DPS trooper denied her entry, even when she explained her position at the school. Heid spotted a Port Arthur Police car nearby. The driver, who knew her, walked over to see what was going on.

Heid explained that she had left the school's servers behind and needed to get them. The officer interceded. This lady is a first responder and must be allowed to pass through the blockade, he said.

The trooper let her through.

As she drove the roads that were as familiar to her as the hallways in her home, Heid was heartbroken at what she saw. The town she loved was almost unrecognizable. Power lines and broken poles blocked the roadways. Tanks from the nearby refineries and rows of debris rested against splintered homes on the road. Waves carried battered boats far from the sea, depositing them, along with other debris, inland.

More than 95 percent of the town's structures were destroyed or badly damaged, hers among them.

Heid's heart pounded as she pulled up to the school. It was still standing, but the storm had taken its toll.

The two-story building was protected by an outer wall built four years earlier to withstand a category 4 hurricane. It seemed mostly intact, though the wind had lifted the roof and blown water in. Mold and mildew already were creeping across the carpet and up walls.

At least the building was still standing, she thought. The gymnasium and auditorium, which sat at ground level, didn't fare as well. The gym floor had buckled, and water flooded the auditorium. Both structures were uninhabitable.

The main building had an emergency generator that was supposed to kick in when the power failed. But, as so many emergency responders and business owners would learn, hurricanes don't give a damn about such things. A nearby company's work trailer crashed into a main gas pipeline entry into Sabine Pass, and workers had to shut the gas supply down.

"Otherwise this building would have come up, and it wouldn't have gotten all the mold and mildew that kept us out of school for almost six weeks," Heid said. "We could have saved a lot of money."

Heid picked up the school's four servers and put them in her car. For the next few weeks, they would go wherever she went, including back and forth to Kemah.

Heid hadn't asked to take a leadership role, but it quickly became apparent that it would fall to her to guide her community through the devastating aftermath of the storm. Although the town is officially part of much larger Port Arthur, it maintains a distinct identity. With only a few businesses and a post office, the school became the logical center of the town – and Heid was going to make sure her citizens' needs were met first.

When word got out how hard Sabine Pass was hit, relief groups, including the Salvation Army and Red Cross, began bringing in supplies. With no designated distribution point, people would pull up to the four-way stop sign and lay things out on the ground on a tarpaulin. Heid and her husband watched as people from outside the community drove up, grabbed water, cleaning supplies and masks, then headed out of Sabine Pass back toward Port Arthur.

It was clear some kind of control was needed to make sure the supplies donated specifically for the residents of Sabine Pass stayed in the community. The next day, Heid inspected the shop building across the street from the school. It was full of mud but the roof was intact, which would provide some shelter from the sun. Heid, Tom Butler, the school's maintenance instructor, and his sister, a teacher, both of whom also were staying in Kemah and driving back and forth, mudded out the building and opened what became known as Sabine-Mart. All this was done with only a generator and a cell phone. It would be weeks before electricity was restored.

Guiseppe Barranco, a photojournalist with The Port Arthur News, had been on the job for less than a year when Rita hit. He was looking for photos that would best convey the destruction the storm had brought when it hit him that Sabine Pass was a logical choice.

"It took me a couple of days to get down there. It was like a ghost town," he said.

Barranco drove to the maintenance building and watched Heid as she directed workers. Impressed by her organizational skills and the obvious respect she earned from those assisting her, he assumed she was a high-ranking official in charge of relief operations.

"Because I hadn't been on the job long, I had no clue who she was," he said.

Barranco asked her if she was an official and who she was with.

"I'm the principal of the school."

"About that time, a small group came up to her and said, 'Kristi,' we have this problem, and this problem, and this problem.' She would say, 'This is what we're going to do. Put this stuff over here and that stuff over there.' She would just rattle off ways to solve the problems," Barranco said. "I was blown away. I told her, 'You really know your community and what's going on.'"

"People figured out I was the contact person and my phone rang constantly," Heid said. "We'd get calls, 'What do you need?' We began to organize the donations. You never knew what was coming, but stuff was coming in every day. We had tents, blankets, lanterns, batteries, food and water. A guy came from East Texas with a trailer full of stuff that had come to them. They didn't need it, but he said he knew we did."

Heid and Tom Butler built some impressive muscles unloading the much-needed supplies under tough conditions. The heat, humidity and mosquitoes were brutal. She didn't mind. Working was therapy. As she watched people come and pick up supplies, she noticed that they lingered, standing in groups, talking about what they had lost and asking their neighbors how they had fared. The sharing of experiences and focusing on the hardships they had in common helped begin the healing.

One afternoon, a worker from Ford Park called to ask Heid what they needed. Heid, who was "huffing and puffing" trying to unload one truck while yet another was pulling in, said, "Unless you've got a forklift, you can't help me."

Heid hung up. The next morning at 7:30, a truck showed up with a forklift.

Heid is grateful for the support of everyone who helped make sure her community wasn't forgotten, including Judge Griffith.

"Carl was instrumental in focusing on the needs of Sabine Pass. He had someone call me every day and come out and check on us. That was good because we didn't have any idea how to approach those big issues he was handling for us."

One morning, Heid was busy unloading a truck when she heard a helicopter overhead. It was Senator John Cornyn, who had flown in to see the damages. The pilot brought the 'copter down on the school's baseball field.

"We kept working, unloading a truck. The next thing we know, up comes a whole group of people. Senator Cornyn, Judge Griffith and one of the main guys from Valero walked up. Judge Griffith wanted to introduce them to me," Heid said.

Governor Rick Perry also toured Sabine Pass.

All the hubbub had an unexpected benefit. It kept Heid from focusing on her own losses. Because her home sits across the street from the school and the storm had pushed in from the north, the school had offered some protection, but couldn't stop the flying debris.

"My house was brick, built up on four foot chain wall. My property is 6 feet above sea level. So my house was 11 feet above sea level. That kept flood water from getting in, but we had roof damages so I had driving rain. Our house was better than most, but we had a lot of damage."

Heid considered herself lucky.

"We had never had a Rita in our generation – or the older folks here either. Rita was pretty tough on everybody. This is a very hard-working community. It's not a lot of rich people and there isn't a lot of money here. It's families living payday to payday. Not a lot of people had insurance. You began to see those things come out and hear the stories. Some didn't know what they were going to do."

"But," she continued, "the great thing you saw was the response from people. Several groups stood out. The Baptist men came in and did the dirtiest work here. They mudded out homes and pulled wet sheet rock out. I didn't realize people did that. They set up a shower trailer and washer and dryer trailer for people to use. Their kinship and support was really great for this community. They were awesome.

"And the Taiwanese came in and helped out with support and monetary gift cards for folks. They were very generous with $500 cards to help people get back on their feet. The Mormon group came in, and they were fabulous. They handed out food and stayed here in horrible conditions. It was hot, snakes were out, and the mosquitoes were horrible. I can't say enough about Salvation Army. They just didn't go away. The response from outside was amazing."

Once other groups began helping out and the initial distribution process was under control, Heid turned her energy back to her school. She knew if the community was going to survive, the school had to be open and functioning. She started tracking reports of how other schools were faring. Port Arthur, 13 miles away, had only 50 percent of the district's students show up the first day of school after the storm.

"I was very worried. Can we survive? We were trying so desperately to do what we could."

The day Sabine Pass School opened its doors six weeks after Rita, 83 percent of the students showed up.

"It was beautiful. There was a lot of media here, and the kids were happy. During those six weeks, parents had called saying they didn't know what to do. Should they put their kids in another school? I told them to do whatever felt comfortable. But I already had plans to catch the students up."

Heid submitted a written plan to the Texas Education Agency on how the school planned to make up the six weeks to avoid losing funding and meet the education requirements for the students. Her plan was, she believes, unique among districts heavily affected by the storm.

"A group of us brainstormed. We thought it would be hard on our community for the kids to have to go to school during the Christmas holidays after everything they had been through. And parents needed their kids at home to help get things put back in order. So we converted our day into minutes and converted that into what the state says you have to do in a day. We found we already go about 36 minutes more a day than you need to. We converted that time back into hours and then days and we had more time in than you have to, even with that six weeks off."

She sent in the plan and held her breath. The TEA accepted it and told the district it would not have to make up any additional days because of their already extended regular school days.

"When all was said and done, we were a recognized school for that year. We were very proud of that. Our staff was fantastic."

When Hurricane Ike hit near Galveston on Sept. 13, 2008, the school staff took everything they had learned and put it into practice while the school was shut down for six weeks once again. That year, the school earned an exemplary rating.

"This school is what this community thrives around. It is the hub of the community," Heid said. "This was our home, our school, and we were going to take care of it."

Heid, who searched for any way she could find to get aid for the school, had an inspired idea. She called the producers of the ABC television reality show, "Extreme Home Makeover." Producers told Heid there was so much devastation they couldn't single out one home to rebuild.

"I was so aggravated," Heid laughed. "The producer said, 'but...I want to talk about a special we're doing on Hurricane Rita."

The show was looking at the most hard hit areas – Florida, Mississippi, Louisiana and Texas – and deciding what they could do that would have the most impact on a community. Heid told the producer that the fire station had been destroyed. She also told them about the school's auditorium, which was an important gathering place for the residents of Sabine Pass. Each Thanksgiving, for example, five different churches in Sabine Pass hold a joint service during which they collect an offering to help folks in need throughout the year. The money goes to such things as paying for prescriptions and utility bills for seniors on a fixed income.

The show "took over" Sabine Pass for a week. While they worked on rebuilding the fire station and the school auditorium, producers sent Heid and the school's theater students to New York, where they spent a day at The Juilliard School, saw the Broadway show, "Phantom of the Opera," and had hair and makeup done for professional head shots for a portfolio. The kids came home in time to participate in "the reveal," where everyone sees the building makeovers for the first time.

Few faces didn't have tears as they celebrated one more milestone in the recovery of a community that proved it might have been battered, but it was not – and would not long be – broken.

Chapter Eleven

Newton and Jasper Counties

Truman Dougharty always heard that the Good Lord
won't put any more on a person than he can stand. Hurricane Rita challenged his faith – and took him as close to a breakdown as he ever wants
to be.

Dougharty is what old-timers call the salt of the earth. He lives his
life by a simple code; do what's right, always tell the truth, and take your
responsibilities seriously. Dougharty became a Texas State Trooper and
spent 27 years upholding the law and protecting citizens while going
after the bad guys. He retired from law enforcement in 1993, saying he'd
had "enough of the pistol-packing business." Not long after his son was
killed in an auto accident, Dougharty decided to run for judge of Newton County, a job his son had encouraged him to seek. In 1999, he beat
out four other candidates.

While rural, largely poor counties without large cities faced many
of the same problems as their larger counterparts after Rita, they had
the additional burden of fewer resources and less experience with hurricanes. Few have fire departments; those that do depend completely on
volunteers. For most of the counties north of the coastline, hurricane
preparedness had been limited to managing traffic for those whose

evacuation route took them through.

Before Katrina, none of the counties north of the coast had experienced the crisis of fuel unavailability and traffic that came to a virtual
standstill for hours, as it did during Rita. They hadn't had to deal with
evacuees whose cars – and tempers – overheated, putting children, the
elderly and medically vulnerable at special risk. They hadn't worried
about stores selling out of water and food during 100-degree temperatures. Although officials had heard the horror stories of Katrina, three
weeks didn't allow time to call meetings, discuss whether emergency
plans should be expanded, and then appoint task leaders for the job.

Newton County, with a population of 15,000, stretches along the
border between Texas and Louisiana. Newton, the county seat, is its only
incorporated city. It's one of longest counties in the state, stretching 90
miles from Toledo Bend Lake on the north to Deweyville on the south,
covering 938 square miles.

During his years as judge, the plain-spoken Dougharty has encountered more than his share of disasters while overseeing the workings of a
poor county with limited resources.

"Tropical Storm Allison like to have washed us off with 14 inches of
rain. We housed 450 evacuees from Hurricane Katrina. We had Hurricanes Gustav, Humberto and Ike. We had four floods on the Sabine
River, 17,000 acres burn in a fire with five homes destroyed. We've had
three tornadoes. Some of it I want to forget forever. But I tell you, Rita
was the worst."

Until Rita, Dougharty's only brush with a hurricane came when his
family evacuated from Brazoria County for Hurricane Carla and came to
Newton County when he was in high school. The city experienced wind
and rain, but no real damage.

Newton County is a place where people from Galveston, Freeport
and even New Orleans go to escape a hurricane, not experience one. It
used to be far enough, but hurricanes like Rita don't hold to tradition.

When Rita threatened Southeast Texas, Dougharty kept in close contact with the other county judges, sitting in during conference calls with
the state. As he watched Rita grow into a monster Category 5 hurricane
600 miles across, he issued a joint mandatory evacuation, the first in his
county's history.

Dougharty, his district attorney, auditor, treasurer, commissioners
and several other county employees stayed at the county jail during the
storm, as did all the city and county police officers and state troopers.

For the first time in his life, Dougharty slept in a jail's drunk tank. Others slept in offices and the prisoner holding tank.

The jail is a one-story building with sturdy concrete walls. During the height of the storm, Dougharty placed his outstretched palm against the glass front door and felt the 116-mile-per-hour winds push it in three to four inches. Like everyone else who could do nothing but sit and wait for morning to come, he worried about what he would find at daylight.

"Everyone just buckled down," he said. "We watched roofing and tin flying down the street. If you had been outside, it would have cut you to pieces."

Newton is about 95 miles inland from the Gulf of Mexico, as the crow flies, so it was noon before the judge figured the wind gusts had died down enough that they could safely venture outside. The town looked as if a can of Silly String had exploded. Downed power lines criss-crossed the streets, and poles teetered precariously.

Dougharty wasn't sure how many people had evacuated and was worried about those who stayed behind. There was no electricity, and cell phone towers had blown down, cutting off communication. Without radio capability, he couldn't find out how the south end of the county had fared. He sent deputies with chain saws to clear the roads enough to get through to check on them.

"Everybody don't evacuate when you want them to," he said. "So we have to cut our way in and see if anyone needs medical attention. We turned the civic center into an emergency room. The State Department of Health finally got us four ambulances so people could get in here and get treated. St. Luke's Hospital in the Woodlands sent us a doctor who came on his own time and stayed to treat people at no cost. A bunch of us caught colds, and he even treated us. They also donated medical supplies."

On Saturday afternoon, the Department of Public Safety sent troopers to East Texas, and they took Dougharty on a helicopter tour. As he flew across the county, he spotted wide slashes of destruction where tornados had touched down, splintering everything in the way.

"We are a heavily-wooded county. There were a lot of trees down on houses and barns. The city lost all its water and sewer. It was just a big nightmare."

Never having been through a hurricane, Dougharty wasn't familiar with the "72-hour push," those cruel first days when local officials have to aggressively pursue government help for debris cleanup at 100 percent reimbursement.

"I didn't even know it existed," he said.

An empathetic county judge in Florida who must have read or seen one of the several media reports quoting Dougharty's frustration wanted to help. He called a surprised Dougharty and told him, "We've been through a lot of these. Here are some things you need to know."

He told Dougharty about the 72-hour push, the blue roof campaign and other available services.

"What amazed me is when FEMA got here, they didn't mention any of those things to me," he said. "They send them to help. You'd think they would sit down and say,' Here's what you can do and what you can't do.'"

Dougharty was desperate for generators, but couldn't secure any. He put in requests through the Governor's Office of Emergency Management in Austin but became frustrated with the "mountains of paperwork" and subsequent wait.

"There were too many people with too many requests. They couldn't fill them. First they had to procure the generators. Then when they get them they say they have to be engineered. Carl Griffith had always been good to help us, so I called him. I said, 'Man, I need some generators. Do you have anyone who can assess our building to satisfy the FEMA folks?' He sent an electrician down to check the sites. Well, FEMA didn't like that. They wanted their own folks. I think the site got engineered three times. They wouldn't accept the city engineer or Carl's guy."

Luckily, a kind soul came to Dougharty's rescue.

"We saw a truck towing a generator through town. We flagged him down and asked. 'Where did you get this generator? We need to get our water and sewer back up."

The man told Dougharty he was with AT&T in Houston – and they had an acre filled with generators. He gave the judge a number to call. "Just come get them," the business owner told him. Dougharty sent trucks, along with a deputy he instructed to tag all the generators and log them in so the county could be sure they all were accounted for and returned.

"They knew we needed them because I had pled my case," Dougharty said. "They deserve credit for that. I will never forget what they did. They didn't charge us a cent for them."

When the FEMA worker finally arrived, he did everything he could to help them, Dougharty said, maybe more than the strict rules permitted.

"He tried to expedite the process and help us cut a few corners and get some relief," Dougharty said. "He was only here a few days before they sent him somewhere up north. They would only stay a couple of days, and then FEMA would send someone else in and you had to update the new crew. It made no sense."

The long days and unresolved needs sent local officials' frustrations soaring. At one point Newton County Sheriff Joe Walker threatened to throw the FEMA "head guy" in jail.

"They finally resolved the situation, and the gentleman got sent on somewhere else," Dougharty said.

By Saturday afternoon, Texas Parks and Wildlife sent game wardens equipped with chain saws to help clear the roads. They were a welcome sight, Dougharty said, and he will never forget their efforts. They were the first ones out in the morning, and the last ones in at night.

"They were my saving grace. They loaded up their trucks with food and walked in to hand-deliver meals to folks. When you saw them at the end of the day, they were the dirtiest people you saw. They weren't afraid to work."

Close to 200 Texas game wardens worked in tandem with regional wardens familiar with the backwoods roads that wind through the county into remote areas. TPWD Division District Leader Gary Calkins of Jasper, along with 12 district wildlife employees, came in at the request of the Jasper-Newton-Sabine Counties Multi-Jurisdictional Emergency Management Center. They helped with search and rescue and went house to house to check on residents. In one day alone, they delivered 2,992 bags of ice, 1,540 MREs and 778 cases of water throughout five counties in East Texas.

The U.S. Forest Service sent in an incident command team to help with planning and recovery.

Col. Pete Flores, TPWD law enforcement director, noted after the storm that Katrina "grabbed and held international news headlines for weeks" while public attention for the hard-hit rural counties quickly dissipated.

"Rural populations are more scattered and broad, not as large and concentrated as in the cities," he said. "But needs of the people are the same. They need help, and we'll provide it, under the direction of our governor."

Dougharty's list of heroes includes the Salvation Army, which was the first group to show up and attend all the meetings, Texas game wardens, the Texas Department of Public Safety, Texas Forest Service and "some counties out west that sent deputies in because all our local counties had their own problems to deal with."

Because Dougharty hadn't known about or pursued help during the 72-hour push, the county had to pay for everything, Dougharty said. He kept meticulous records.

"My treasurer followed me around with a tablet and wrote down the day and time and everything that happened. When they came back and audited us, I could pull out the book and say, 'This is exactly what the man said. This is what was authorized.'"

Dougharty said Rita taught him that "You'd better be self sufficient. You'd better start trying to get your things in order and take notes and be ready if it happens again. The help is going to take awhile. It's such a paperwork jungle."

In those dark hours when Dougharty had plunged to his lowest emotional point, he felt an acute responsible for what his citizens endured, and he took it hard when he couldn't make things happen the way he wanted.

"Everyone thinks a county judge can do anything. I wish I could. You are in an elected position and people are expecting you to take care of them. But you have limitations like everyone else. When you are a poor county, for instance, you can't just call up and order generators without knowing what you will get reimbursed for. I would have broke the county."

The fight for reimbursement remains a sore spot for Dougharty, who believes his county was shortchanged compared to nearby counties who received much larger sums.

"They came out with a list of counties and how much they would be reimbursed. One county had $30 million, and they had Newton down for $2.5 million. I told them, what is wrong with you people? We got hit just as hard. I'm a Democrat but finally, I called Congressman Kevin Brady and Senator John Cornyn, both Republicans, and told them I needed help. They finally come through for me. I got a letter saying there was a big error, and I would be getting a letter from FEMA saying it would be increased to $11.5 million. They said they didn't know what caused the error."

Despite frustrations, anxiety, and yes, anger over the way he believes his county was shortchanged, Dougharty focused on putting the biggest challenge of his life behind him.

"Good wins out over evil. Just stay the course and do what you are supposed to do. It usually pays off. I have to speak for the people of my county and protect them. That's what I do."

After Rita, Dougharty considered retiring. The only thing that stopped him was his sense of duty. The historic Newton county courthouse burned on his watch five years before Rita hit, he said, and he wanted to stay around for the rebuilding and see his county into its new home.

While Dougharty was fighting for equity for his county, Judge Joe Folk of Jasper was facing the same challenges. Folk, now retired, was aided by Jasper-Newton-Sabine County Emergency Management and Homeland Security Coordinator Billy Ted Smith.

Folk had taken Smith's recommendation to issue the first ever mandatory evacuation for southern Jasper County on Thursday, Sept. 21, followed by evacuation for the rest of the county the next day. The county still had around 1,000 Katrina evacuees and knew from past hurricanes that their area would be receiving an influx of people fleeing Rita.

"Years back, everyone evacuated to Jasper, including people from Louisiana," Smith said. "During Hurricane Andrew in 1992, we ended up with close to 8,000 people here. After that, when (officials) re-evaluated and looked at the risk, they pushed the surge zone on up to the Evadale and Deweyville areas. Since then, they've moved it even further in."

Jasper County officials had done everything they could to be as prepared as possible to protect the county's 36,800 folks. They signed up for and attended all training classes they could find. Smith is proud of the fact that Jasper, along with neighboring Nacogdoches County, both were certified by the State of Texas as storm ready.

Still, he said, "you always run into things you never dreamed you'd face."

Around 30 percent of the county evacuated. Those who left chose to go early, Smith said.

"They'd been through the traffic nightmare before."

Like elsewhere in Southeast and East Texas, ambulances, gasoline and generators were in short supply. Hospitals and nursing homes shut down and evacuated their patients as best they could, getting help from Stat Care EMS.

County officials set up the emergency operations center at Jasper's Fire Station. The storm hit around 2 a.m. and continued to hover for three to four hours. Once it calmed down, Smith and Folk kept waiting for the back side to hit. It never came.

During the storm, owner Mike Lout of radio station KJAS stayed on the air, broadcasting information from the station's links to the National Weather Service and Emergency Management Weather Information Network. When he called Folk and asked the judge to say a few words to the citizens, Folk didn't hesitate.

"Mike, who is the mayor of Jasper now, wanted me reassure everyone that things were being taken care of. I don't remember what I said, other than things were being looked after and we had rescue teams if they were needed."

Considering the scope of a storm coming so close on the heels of Katrina, Smith and Folk have no problem handing out praise for those who came to their aid.

"We were getting food and water shipments from FEMA. They responded pretty quickly. They sent the National Guard in, and they were here at our pleasure until we released them," Folk said. "The game wardens from the Texas Department of Parks and Wildlife were excellent. They were out in rural areas every night keeping the curfew and passing out water and food. Our county employees were steadfast, and our citizens are our heroes. People were out helping each other. The physical help was outstanding."

What Folk and Smith did have a problem with was the inability to get help from the American Red Cross because of the automatic assistance zip code program FEMA began after Katrina that proved to be a failure. Even the President's disaster declaration didn't help. Only people living in specific zip codes were granted automatic help. The only option for those outside those codes was to later appeal.

That provoked immense frustration and resentment from folks in Jasper County who had been on site helping Hurricane Katrina victims receive aid. Those who watched the debit cards and vouchers being handed out, then helped organize airline flights and book long-term hotel rooms for the evacuees in advance of Rita felt abandoned.

"Everyone saw how the government was helping. The citizens of Southeast Texas thought they should have some help too. But it didn't happen that way. FEMA treated the folks from Louisiana and Mississippi totally different than they did our folks here in Texas," Smith said.

"People would be standing in line five to six hours just to be told, 'You are not eligible because you didn't have a disaster declaration in your county.' That wasn't true," Folk said. "We did that early on. They had no record of it. We ended up sending a copy of our declaration, along with the state's and one from the President. We mailed it to the Red Cross national headquarters. It was several days after the disaster before they came in and had a meeting with us."

Folk, who said he got a "little emotional," took exception to the Red Cross representative's assurances that they were doing the same for Rita's victims as Katrina's.

"It wasn't so – and I told him so. He got unhappy. I told him, you can say what you want, but we know what you did for Katrina because we were right here with them."

Folk said he had no problem with the local Red Cross chapters, which he respects. "They worked really hard. If it was left up to the local Red Cross, we would have been taken care of."

Folk and Smith say the recovery battle would have been much more difficult, if not impossible, without the help of their elected officials.

"Both our senators, John Cornyn and Kay Bailey Hutchison, came here and also sent staff to meet with us. I don't know of a thing Congressman Kevin Brady could do that he didn't do for us. He was here on a regular basis, not just once or twice. He was here to see about us every time you turned around," Folk said. "We were concerned when he was running for Congress because he was from the city (The Woodlands). He said 'Don't worry. I won't forget about these deep East Texas woods.' And he was true to his word."

Chapter Twelve

Incident Management

Disasters don't come along every day – or every year

– and emergency management and response are only a small part of
elected and appointed officials' jobs. Their expertise is focused on the
day-to-day fulfillment of their duties. Emergency response requires
intense, on-going specialized training outside the capability of most local
and regional city and government folks. Emergency medical technicians
have to know how to treat victims of accidents and illness. Law enforcement officers have to know how to handle people-based incidents. Fire
departments have to be trained to respond to fires, medical crises and
other types of emergencies.

Today, one of the most recognized and successful approaches to
handling disasters is the Incident Command System. Back in the 1970s,
a string of widespread fires in Southern California weren't managed as
well as involved agencies would have liked. To assess what went wrong
and how it could be improved, county, state and federal fire agencies met
to explore opportunities to increase their effectiveness.

At the time, many of the agencies had their own system of communication codes, language and command structure, making communication
between agencies disjointed and leaving openings for confusion. What

they needed, the agencies decided, was one uniform system for emergency incident response.

That was the beginning of NIMS, the National Incident Management System. Incidents are categorized according to complexity, from the lowest level (V) to the highest (I). Hurricane Rita was Type I.

During the Rita response, participants came from several agencies, including USDA Forest Service, U.S. Department of the Interior Bureau of Land Management, U.S. Department of the Interior National Park Service, and Benton County, Wash.

Darren Kennedy and Natural Resource Specialist Beth Rode work for the U.S. Forest Service as Fire Management Officers with the Columbia River Gorge National Scenic Area in Hood River, Ore. Both came to Southeast Texas during Hurricane Rita.

When an interagency incident management team comes to an area for the first time, it often is met with a guarded response. Sometimes, personnel encounter subtle hostility from local leaders who see them as outsiders trying to take over. Understandably, local responders have a huge emotional stake in what happens during the recovery process and feel protective about their roles.

What they often don't realize is NIMS adheres to the belief that all incidents begin and end locally. Rather than taking command away from state and local authorities, NIMS and IMTs are valuable resources with a proven standardized structure that can help all responders work together more effectively, the Forest Service says. No city or county has a full-time staff adequate to deal with a large-scale emergency on the scope of Hurricane Rita. Even the most prepared teams can become overwhelmed.

Incident Management Teams don't supersede local and state management; they greatly increase their capability, Kennedy said. Interagency incident management teams have responded to hurricanes and other natural disasters for years, but have been under utilized, in his opinion. That changed the day terrorists flew planes into the World Trade Center and the Pentagon on 9/11.

Several IMTs were dispatched to the World Trade Center a couple of days after the attack. The New York City Fire Department referred to them as "forestry volunteers." By the time the teams left, FDNY had become believers. In 2002, the nation's largest fire department began shadowing teams to learn more about how they managed incidents, said Kennedy, who worked with FDNY in the Boundary Waters Canoe Wilderness Area in Northern Minnesota and Northwestern Montana.

Today, FDNY has a Type I Incident Management Team of its own.

Kennedy was assigned as the point of contact for the Port Arthur Emergency Operations Center, where he worked closely with John Owens for the next two weeks.

While first responders from Southeast Texas often refer to the Rita team as "The Forest Service Guys," the team drew members from other agencies. While the bulk of the team was Forest Service employees, during Hurricane Rita team members also came from the Bureau of Indian Affairs, Bureau of Land Management and local-level fire jurisdictions from other parts of the country.

"At the time, the deputy incident commander of our team was a Benton County (Washington State) Fire Chief. My point here is that we refer to our teams as interagency incident management teams because truly, that's what they are," Kennedy said.

Beaumont's first female Fire Chief Anne Huff is a believer in the incident management approach to disasters. In 2005, when Rita hit, she was the chief training officer for the department. The first class she organized was incident command training. Although the class was structured for small-scale events, Huff believes command is command, no matter what size or form an emergency takes.

"Once you know the principles and are able to apply them, they apply to the smaller incident all the way up to the biggest one. Large scale incident command is structured to get things done while minimizing the chance of people getting hurt," Huff said.

For Hurricane Rita, Huff and Deputy Chief Chris Singler handpicked six fire department personnel to work with them at the Jefferson County EOC in Port Arthur, where she was assigned to be the planning section chief for Hurricane Rita response.

Later, when the EOC moved to Edison Plaza, Huff asked Griffith to include an NIMS overhead team as part of the resources he was requesting from the state.

Within 72 hours, the team was on site at Ford Park, assisting with the logistics of distribution of supplies delivered by the state. Huff met up with Kennedy and his team and shadowed them.

"They were so gracious. They brought me through every one of the sections and answered anything I wanted answered. They gave me materials, including CDs with their computer program that tracks every request when it arrives. At the end of the event, whatever it is, from a wildfire to a hurricane to a Super Bowl, they can run a report and tell you what everything cost."

Huff was impressed with the confidence with which the team operated. "Nobody was stressed. They are used to doing it, and it's what they do. That was the two most valuable training days I've ever had, seeing the system and how it works in real life."

Jeff Phillips, a Beaumont Fire Department Captain who now is the department's emergency operations planning section chief, said he believes the county's emergency management would have been more focused and widespread if incident management training had been made available prior to Hurricane Rita.

That didn't happen, he believes, because of general complacency that settled in because of the lack of any serious hurricanes for decades.

"We hadn't had an emergency like that since 1988. Everybody had gotten complacent as far as hurricanes and emergency management were concerned. It was pretty much an afterthought. And (Huff's) budget at the time kept getting raided. There is a possibility that training was available, but there weren't funds. After Katrina, there weren't federal funds for that either. She had trouble getting it approved for us to get trained. And that's precisely what we needed."

During Rita, Phillips worked with Points of Distribution (PODS), where critical supplies such as ice, water and food were distributed. It fell to the fire department to take care of that, rather than focusing on other critical needs. Now, Phillips said, the department knows all it has to do is call in an Incident Management Team for help.

"The Forest Service will completely run the PODS. We had no knowledge of that. I'm a big fan of the Forestry Service. They know how to do emergency management."

"When I arrived at the Port Arthur EOC I came in unannounced, which gave me the opportunity to stand aside and watch the operation for some 10-15 minutes prior to introducing myself to John Owens," Kennedy recalled. "The EOC had been set up in a wide hallway outside of the conference rooms at the motel. Several tables had been set up in a row where different functions were attempting to meet the needs of the incident. There was no electricity and therefore no lights or air conditioning. In that confined space with outside temps reaching into the middle 90's, temperatures inside were likely well above 100. Somewhere in the neighborhood of 20-30 people were actively attempting to address specific issues such as fuel (where to obtain it, how to transport it...), power, (when, where and how it would be restored), emergency response (fire and medical calls), and establishing food, water and ice distribution sites and law enforcement. Both state and local were heavily engaged in maintaining closures, patrolling for looters and other general security matters. The short version is that in my opinion John and his team were chasing all of the correct priorities."

Kennedy said when it comes to incident management, he did recognize some opportunities for improvement. In his words:

"One, there were numerous people assigned to chase the same or similar issues. As an example, I listened to three conversations (law enforcement, fire & EMS, and public works) related to the fuel issue. Each one of these groups was attempting to take care of their own, which is good, yet the effort could have been more effectively organized.

"Two, it was obvious to me that most of the people I was watching were extremely tired and tempers were short, etc. When you're engaged in an incident for the long haul, sleep deprivation can be a killer. I learned later that most of these folks hadn't slept since the evacuations began three or four days earlier.

"Three, the work space was dismal and therefore less productive than it could have been."

After observing the team for a while, Kennedy introduced himself to Owens, explaining that his team was set up at Ford Park in Beaumont, and that he would be the liaison to the Port Author EOC.

"My direction when I left Ford Park was simply that – to provide liaison and coordination between the Port Arthur EOC and the Beaumont EOC. John was very pleased that I was there, which frankly surprised me, and he pulled his core team together for a quick meeting."

When Owens introduced Kennedy as the "point man" for the team that was coming in to relieve them, Kennedy knew he was in trouble, he said. He had some disappointing news to deliver.

"We went around the room for introductions, and his team briefed me regarding what they had going on. Then it was my turn. To put it mildly, the news that I was the only member of my, or any team that was coming to Port Arthur, was not well received. I later learned that John and his team had been requesting a team for three days. I explained that my team had arrived with some 35-40 people and that we had been tasked with supporting Jefferson County and that the bulk of that work (supporting the Beaumont EOC, FEMA and coordinating with the Army National Guard, Red Cross etc.) was in Beaumont. I told the group that I would request additional help from my team, but that I could not guarantee anything."

At the end of the meeting, Kennedy shared his observation with Owens and made several recommendations. Within 24 hours, a "very receptive" Owens had most of the recommendations in place, Kennedy said.

Kennedy offered coaching regarding structure on things like establishing clear schedules for briefings and chain of command.

"For example, all logistical support needed to be coordinated through the now established Logistics Section Chief and so on and so forth with the Finance Section Chief and the Planning Section Chief. I was very impressed with John and his group. They were very responsive to suggestions and knowledgeable and professional. Within two days the EOC was running as smoothly as could be expected."

By day two, Kennedy had some good news to share. His request for additional help from his team was answered. He was joined by Beth Rode, who worked as a Type III Plans Section Chief; Theresa Wright, who helped with finances; and Bob Thomas, who assisted with logistics.

"There were others from my team who popped in and out to assist us, but those mentioned were the core group from PNW Team 2. Beth did an outstanding job of organizing, planning, producing Incident Action Plans and running the briefings and meetings. We did request and receive additional assistance from the wildland fire community in the form of individuals and crews to run and staff Points of Distribution for water, ice and food, some of them coming from as far away as Alaska. This allowed local fire fighters and EMS personnel to return to their normal duties of responding to fire and EMS emergencies," Kennedy said.

Not all the restoration work came from the EOC, Kennedy added.

"The power companies had swarmed the area attempting to restore the electrical grid. The US Coast Guard was patrolling the waterways and containing hazardous material spills. Work on repairing the refineries to get them fully operational was ongoing. And all of it had potential to impact health and public safety. John and I talked about these circumstances and extended invitations to these entities / organizations to attend our planning sessions and briefings. By day four or five we had representatives from Total, U.S. Coast Guard, public works and the power company in regular attendance."

From that point forward, Kennedy said, his role turned into that of advisor, where he said, "I'd like to believe that I helped what I now viewed as our team avoid some of the financial pitfalls and political hazards that go hand in hand with large incidents."

Chapter Thirteen

In the Dark

Katrina brought an unprecedented challenge to elec-
trical provider Entergy Texas, Inc. which serves parts of Arkansas, Louisiana, Mississippi and Texas. The severe flooding and wind damage left an 1.1 million customers without power throughout a 37,000 square mile area. The majority, 800,000, were in Louisiana, with another 300,000 in Mississippi.

Twenty-six days later, Rita created a similar crisis, bringing infrastructure to a standstill as she incapacitated the electrical supply across southeast Texas and southwestern Louisiana. Her winds and tornados flattened or snapped utility poles. Thousands of trees and limbs fell on power lines, bringing down transmission stations. When all was said and done, more than three quarters of a million customers were without power, 286,000 of them in Texas. A dozen generation units were offline, 343 transmission lines and 436 substations were out of service and more than 9,000 distribution poles were broken.

"In addition to getting the lights back on with Katrina, we also had a company that was devastated corporately. Our headquarters was in New Orleans, and New Orleans was under water. The bank we used was in New Orleans. Their computer system was damaged. So we had questions like, how do we pay employees? If you get direct deposit and your bank is not operating, what do you do? Not only that, but some of the employees don't get their paychecks deposited directly. Where are they? How do you find them?" said Entergy Texas President and CEO Joe Domino.

"Before Katrina, people evacuated and in a couple of days it was over. This was a long process. We learned that when your corporate finance, corporate transmission planning and corporate organization is all located in one place that is hit by a natural disaster, you're really set back. We diversified geographically. Now, if a disaster hits one place, the entire company is not shut down."

Entergy moved its computer center from Gretna, La. near the corporate office, to Arkansas. They transferred some of the financial staff to the Woodlands, near Houston. Their transmission organization now is based in Jackson, Miss.

With an outage the scope of Hurricane Rita, restoration begins with getting the transmission system – the highway – back together. After transmission comes distribution, then restoration to individual neighborhoods. Decisions are made through a prioritizing process designed to get power restored to the most people in the shortest period of time.

"Assuming that all else is equal, if you are looking at putting a crew on a problem that restores 3,000 people compared to putting that crew on a circuit that restores 300 people, the 300 people stay in the dark longer," Domino said.

Because of the power outages in Louisiana after Katrina, work crews from across the nation already were mobilized nearby. They worked around the clock to finish the work in Louisiana and Mississippi so they could begin restoration efforts for Rita, the second worst storm in the company's history.

Utility companies such as Entergy participate in a mutual assistance organization, sending help when requested by those on the ground in the impacted area. Mobilizing a small army of restoration workers is a massive undertaking, especially when the workforce already is exhausted and materials are in short supply.

Entergy had sent significant resources to New Orleans to help with Katrina. Days before Rita hit, Domino had been visiting his crews south of New Orleans looking at the damage that had occurred there.

"When Rita hit here, the timing was within almost two days of overlapping. We were almost through wrapping up what we could do in Louisiana, since most of it was underwater and there were no people there anyway. We had been working for almost a month, and then we had Rita. Our folks who didn't go to help with Katrina were pulling double duty here. You don't staff up a company in case you might have a hurricane. That's where the relief from other companies helps. We sent contactors plus employees, over 200 people, for Katrina. Our employee count at the time was around 350 for Entergy Texas (not counting contractors). When you put the two together, it was about half our force."

The first question the supporting crews ask is "How many people do you need?" It's a question that can't be answered until the utility company does damage assessment. In heavily wooded areas with hundreds of thousands of trees or limbs down, that means taking to the air.

"The first couple of days after a storm, restoration goes slow, because our effort mainly is on assessing damage. We couldn't get helicopters in the air for Rita for probably 24 hours. Rita hit during the night, and the next afternoon around 4 o'clock we still had squalls, so it was Sunday before we could get people in the air. You don't have a good idea of the damage until 36-48 hours after the storm strikes."

For Rita, finding outside help meant recruiting 13,000 tool workers and more than 4,500 support personnel. More than 130 companies came to Entergy's aid during Katrina and Rita. At the peak of Rita restoration efforts, Entergy had more than 11,000 workers mobilized in Southeast Texas in a tent city, as well as five helicopters, cranes, marsh buggies and other transportation, and heavy equipment. It was a 24-hour operation with crews working 16 hours straight.

"They might get in by 9 p.m." said Entergy's Director of Customer Service Vernon Pierce. "Trucks have to be refueled so that at 6 a.m. they can head out again."

A crew is just the tip of the restoration iceberg, Domino said.

"Now you need fuel, food and water. How do you wash their clothes? What happens if someone cuts their hand and needs stitches? So at our staging sites, which we set up throughout the service area affected by the storm, we have caterers lined up, tents for sleeping, some medical personnel, physician assistants or nurses and people who can provide minor care. There was no electricity, so it was unbearably hot. We try to get hotels if they are available. There's just not enough room for all your folks. You're competing with other organizations. For example, other industries have restoration plans that require bringing people in. Exxon-Mobil, TOTAL – they all are bringing people in. There is a lot of demand for sleeping and eating facilities."

Entergy looked at any and all options for the additional crews, concerned about the brutally hot environment.

"We were utilizing anything we could. The heat was tremendous. We felt for safety reasons we needed to make sure they could get a decent night's sleep and let their bodies recoup from the hard labor. We were sleeping in tents, school and church gyms and fellowship halls, anyplace with air conditioning. The first few nights were pretty rough in those 500-man tents."

Entergy's caterers could at least provide good food for the exhausted crews. They furnished each worker with full breakfasts, box lunches and a hearty meal at night.

Sometimes, it's the things people take for granted that require a bit of ingenuity when nothing around them is normal or simple.

"Let's say a lineman needs his clothes washed. Typically he will have a shirt, pants, underwear and socks. You have 10,000 people. How do you sort that much laundry and get it to the right people? So we use straps that you thread through the neck of the shirt, the leg of the underwear and whatever, put a bag for the socks, and put the person's name on it. Now you have one piece of laundry. It's all in a net that gets washed. Sometimes someone puts in a red shirt and everybody has pink clothes the next day. We don't sort for color," Domino laughed, "but we do give them clean clothes."

Even in such uncomfortable circumstances, Pierce said he observed nothing but good spirits and cooperation from everyone involved. "Employees were just tremendous. I can't say enough about how they rose to the occasion."

When Entergy began restoration efforts, they chose to get a large substation in Lumberton back online. Their goal was to get as far as they could toward Entergy's command center, which also was without power. The first customer to come back on was Walmart.

"Someone gave us a compliment, saying 'That as so smart for y'all to get Walmart back on because they can supply food, gasoline and other essentials'. I said, I sure wish I could take all the credit, but to be quite honest, we were trying to get power to us so we could use our computers to get people's power on quicker from our command center," Domino said.

Communication was critical for staying on track and keeping priorities straight. Every day, key Entergy personnel participated in conference calls with emergency workers and government officials. They would fill officials in on what their crews had accomplished the day before and what their plans were for that day. They then opened up the calls to see what the most critical needs were for everyone else for that day.

"We tried to accommodate those requests, like 'Can you get the water pumps up so we can protect the city from fires? Can you get the sewer lift pumps on? Can you get our emergency command center up?' It was an open, professional dialogue without any pettiness. We worked hard as a team to accommodate those needs," Pierce said.

Entergy also maintained a constant flow of information to the general public through media outlets online, from radio stations like KLVI to newspapers and television stations. Evacuees who were spread throughout the country were making decisions on when to come home based largely on whether they had power. The temperatures were unusually high for September, hovering around 100, plus humidity levels that intensified the heat. People with answering machines would call home several times a day, hoping to hear it pick up.

"I got so much feedback from people telling me how much they appreciated the information they got from KLVI because they were in Tennessee or Arkansas or Florida, and their only contact was the radio station on the internet," Domino said.

After the calls with the media, providing updates on what areas were being restored, Domino would call the area's industrial partners. He was getting a lot of pressure from industry customers in the energy sector, as he was reminded when the Bush administration in Washington called to check on the progress.

"Refineries in this area are very critical, not just to us, but to the nation. We have to work very quickly to get them on because it opens the whole gas supply of the nation. We get calls from the White House wanting to know the status of the refineries. A lot of eyes were watching this area," Pierce said.

As part of informing the public, Pierce and Domino made themselves available to any media requests, despite the chaos around them, knowing how hungry people were for information.

"The day after Rita hit, Channel 12 asked me to come down and do an interview. I go down there and ring the doorbell in the back. No one came. So I opened the door, went in and looked around. Water is running down all this electronic equipment. I meandered my way back to the set and there is Mike Elrod, the station manger, on the set. There was a camera guy and one other person. They said come sit down and we'll interview you. I look terrible with a two-day growth of beard. I came around and sat down in the chair, which is soaking wet. I'm sitting on TV in a puddle of water. I sat there with a stupid smile on my face knowing when I stand up I'm going to look pretty dumb."

Each day, Entergy received endless calls, with the same questions, "When do you think my lights will be back on?"

During Rita, Entergy launched a new mapping program that let customers check to see if power had been restored to their neighborhoods. The dreaded red lines on the map meant service had not been restored. The color everyone wanted to see was green for go. Pierce thinks seeing that they had no power might have helped keep residents from coming back too soon.

While they could provide a general neighborhood timetable for customers, they couldn't guarantee everyone in a particular area would have power restored.

"Many times damage would occur to the system, and we would repair the line going down the road, but someone might have a tree in their yard break a wire to their house and nowhere else. We can't tell house by house who has power. We don't have that technology – but it's coming. It's called Advanced Metering Infrastructure (AMI), and we'll literally be able to map where power has been restored," Domino said.

Entergy has 392,000 customers in Texas. The afternoon of the storm, 280,000 of them were without power. In an astonishing feat, Entergy had 75 percent of those customers back online in 10 days. By October 15, restoration was complete.

"The success of Rita, as far as restoration, would not have happened if not for the employees of this company who are less fortunate than I. They didn't just have a roof blown off, like we did. They had a house missing. And they were still out working to help other people, most of them up to 20 hours a day. That's a sacrifice many people don't realize a lot of our employees made. We tried to help them as best we could with a place to stay and whatever they needed, but they were back here working," Domino said. "And were it not for the employees and the help that came from elsewhere, we wouldn't be talking about it being three weeks to restore power. It would have been a lot longer. The success is to the credit to those dedicated folks who despite the damage they had with their personal situation were working to help others. I am very proud of them. If there were hurricane heroes, they were hurricane heroes."

Pierce is quick to praise those who don't work at Entergy but also put their own lives on hold to help the communities they serve.

"The leadership of this area, elected officials, fire, police, DPS, Coast Guard, state emergency managers – the list goes on and on for those who support the initiatives. I guess I'm patting myself on the back a little because I was part of that, but I'm pretty proud that we rose to the occasion."

Tom Purvis of Motiva was one of the refinery leaders who did what they could to partner with the energy giant.

"The biggest issues were emergency services, and the folks at Entergy did a fine job of addressing the highest priorities first and then keeping people informed. Entergy people from Domino on down were really proactive to reach out to all of us waiting on them to see where they were. They held regular meetings and called us a lot. We had a great relationship. We worked closely with them to do things to help identify issues. Our people were very familiar with the distribution system in South County. They walked the lines and fed that information to Entergy. It was pretty impressive. Industries and communities were well behaved, cooperative and helped where they could. They reached out to neighbors and worked on others' houses as well. That spirit was fabulous," Purvis said.

After Rita, Entergy continued to evaluate restoration efforts from all angles, looking for ways to make future recovery more efficient, safe and comfortable for everyone involved. Obviously, they can't bring in equipment and supplies before the storm, but they can locate what they need and pre-position it in Shreveport and Dallas so they can get it to the affected areas as soon as possible.

Instead of depending on tents, Entergy now contracts with companies that provide bunk trailers to come in as soon as winds subside, providing beds for workers in a comfortable environment. They also have acquired generators they can loan to hotels so they can provide more lodging. Also on standby will be adequate numbers of portapotties.

"There are things we've learned from Rita, and if I had to pick one thing we could have done better, logistics would be it," Pierce said. "And we have made those changes. We are much better prepared for events now."

Pierce said he was impressed by the patience most people showed while waiting for restoration to be complete.

"I talked to a lot of customers during that time, and 99 percent of them were just super. They were living without power, but they knew we were coming. I personally never got into any negative conversations. I had no issues with any of the government officials. I'm pretty proud of Southeast Texas and how well we worked together to come back from a tragedy. That says a lot about the caliber of people here."

Chapter Fourteen

FEMA

Whether it's a simple accident or a major disaster

such as Hurricane Rita, when things go wrong, there is no shortage of finger-pointing. No single agency took more heat after the 2005 hurricane season than the Federal Emergency Management Agency (FEMA). While the agency doesn't dispute its shortcomings during Rita, it does make clear that the general public's misunderstanding of its role contributes to the bad rap it has been fighting since Katrina.

FEMA operates under the authority of the Robert T. Stafford Disaster Relief and Emergency Assistance Act, signed into law Nov. 23, 1988. The Stafford Act was an amendment to the Disaster Relief Act of 1974. It establishes the authority for FEMA's disaster response activities. In other words, FEMA can only do what the act says it can. It does not have autonomy in the decision-making process on how to support an area after a disaster.

FEMA is divided into 10 regions. When it comes to disasters, Region 6 is the indisputable problem child. Seven of the top 10 costliest United States disasters happened in the five states that make up the region: Arkansas, Louisiana, New Mexico, Oklahoma, and Texas.

Katrina holds the dubious distinction of being No. 1 at $28.5 billion in federal funding, and growing, followed by the World Trade Center terrorist attack in New York at $9 billion. The Northridge earthquake of 1994 in California cost $7 billion. Hurricane Rita comes in 4th, with the total still mounting.

"They call us the disastrous region," FEMA Region VI Deputy Administrator Gary Jones, who during Hurricanes Katrina/Rita was designated as both Federal Coordinating Officer and Deputy Principal Federal Official, said. "Historically, with the Oklahoma City bombing in 1995 and the Space Shuttle Columbia explosion in 2003, we've had our fill of disasters. That's why it's key that we have a good close working partnership with our states and all the stakeholders."

Perhaps the most widespread assumption is that FEMA is a first responder with an agency of thousands of full-time employees on standby for federally-declared disasters. Not true.

First of all, FEMA is not a first responder, a misconception that existed prior to Katrina/Rita and which FEMA has battled to correct.

"First responders are those local fire, police, EMS, public works and others who are always on the scene first," Jones said. FEMA does have urban search and rescue teams that can be deployed – but only when requested by the state. "We work through the state on everything we do, through the governor and his or her designated state emergency management director. That allows us to augment the first responders, like we've done on many historical disasters, like the Oklahoma City bombing. Federal urban search and rescue teams work under the supervision of the local incident commander, which is usually under local law enforcement or the fire department. FEMA does not come in and take over and take charge of a disaster."

Instead, FEMA is a part of the overall emergency management team.

"That disaster belongs to that state and local government. When FEMA gets involved at the request of the governor, it is important that we work under that unified command and under the direction of what the state's needs are."

The second part of that misconception is that FEMA is a massive agency ready to go at a moment's notice.

"People think we are like a big fire department. We sit and wait on the next disaster to happen," Jones said.

While disasters are FEMA's No. 1 priority, the agency spends much of its time in mass preparedness, planning, training and exercises with each region's states, Jones said. The federal agency provides billions of grant dollars to state and local agencies, including terrorism grants, to better prepare them to deal with an emergency or disaster.

Jones said that there is "no doubt" Katrina/Rita was a wakeup call for the nation.

"Unfortunately, emergency management and national disasters were not given as much priority as they have today. Since Katrina/Rita this region has grown from 97 to nearly 300 employees."

To complicate matters, prior to Katrina/Rita the Department of Homeland Security (DHS)/FEMA had a hiring freeze on the Disaster Assistance Employee program. Approximately 250 reservists were available to deploy to the disaster. Today, that number has quadrupled to more than 1,000 for Region 6.

As of May 26, 2011 FEMA had 7,382 employees across the country working to support citizens and first responders. At any time, FEMA has at least 1,000 and as many as 9,600 Disaster Assistance Employees available to support disaster-related work.

Because most people need a full-time job, the cadre of DAEs is made up mostly of retirees who have a specific specialty based on their past work experiences. When they are available to work, they log their names in as ready to go. The biggest challenge with DAEs is the temporary job status. At any given time, some are not available, whether sick or on vacation or facing family or other obligations.

Also, DAEs have varying levels and amounts of experience. At any given time, only a third might have expert status. Others have a few disasters under their belts while some might be beginners working their first disaster. Since Hurricanes Katrina and Rita, that experience level has risen considerably.

In response to the less than exemplary handling of the major disasters of the past decade, Congress and FEMA have begun to focus on catastrophic planning. Hurricanes are only one type of disaster for which they must be prepared.

"We handle the garden-variety disaster pretty well in our states in this region, but it's the big national disasters like a Katrina/Rita that require everyone pulling together to make sure our citizens are taken care of when they come in harms way. This is what we call the 'whole community approach,' with emphasis on all everyone, including all citizens, getting trained and responding to support those disaster survivors. Currently, lot of money and emphasis is being put towards catastrophic planning. For example, the New Madrid earthquake fault zone in the central

U.S. takes in about eight states. In our region, Arkansas is part of that seismic zone. There is a considerable amount of money being spent on New Madrid earthquake preparedness in case an earthquake ever occurs, which will be very catastrophic.

"We've come a long way in building up our staffing and in helping train our staffs, just as we promote training state and local responders. We still have a way to go, but the current administration knows the importance of having trained, sufficient staff to do the job when we need to do it," Jones said.

The Stafford Act also outlines how federal money is spent. For example, communities are responsible for debris removal. It is up the local officials to arrange those contracts and to know what constitutes a reasonable cost for debris removal. If they are overcharged by contractors, FEMA can limit reimbursement. In cases of large building demolition or massive debris removal, FEMA will coordinate with the U.S. Army Corps of Engineers, as it did during Rita recovery.

The act also outlines eligibility for reimbursement for such additional expenses as overtime for first responders, necessary equipment and damage repairs to or replacement of public facilities.

FEMA's Individual Assistance Program covers such things as temporary housing during displacement from a home. It also reimburses people for things like medical expenses, funeral expenses and repairs to make a home re-habitable once eligibility is determined. Presently, the maximum grant amount available for Individual Assistance is $30,200.

The public assistance program reimbursement is based on a cost-share percentage. Usually FEMA will pay 75 percent, and the local and state government pays the remaining 25 percent. Occasionally, it can be a 90/10 split.

In the case of Hurricane Katrina, reimbursement hit 100 percent for some expenses. After a prolonged push from U.S. Senators Kay Bailey Hutchison of Texas and Mary Landrieu of Louisiana, Texas was granted the same deal.

During a disaster, FEMA works in partnership with other organizations that are part of the nation's emergency management system. These partners include state, local, and tribal emergency management agencies, the private sector, federal agencies, disability advocates, and volunteer agencies that include the American Red Cross.

One of the most contentious moments at the logistics center at Ford Park during Rita recovery was a battle over generators procured by

FEMA. With all electrical power out and a huge lack of generators for critical first responders, Judge Griffith was working to get generators out as quickly as possible.

Brit Featherston, who had taken a leadership role at the EOC, called Griffith from Ford Park and told him 50 or more generators had been sitting on the lot for at least a day, and FEMA was saying they probably would not move for at least a couple more days.

"What are you talking about?" Griffith asked.

Featherston explained that the Corps of Engineers had to assess each location in all the affected counties before they would release the generators.

"That means they have to talk to every hospital, every commissioner, every police department before they send out a generator," he told Griffith. "You've got to do something."

Although Griffith didn't like leaving the EOC, where pressing issues required his decision making, he left around 4 p.m. on Monday and headed to Ford Park. He met with all the pertinent federal agents and after a heated discussion in which FEMA stood by its decision, Griffith told them they had until 8 p.m. to decide where they were sending the generators.

Griffith, who had had been inundated with calls from officials and first responders throughout the region who didn't have emergency generators for backup power, told FEMA, "This is where you are going to send those generators: the Hardin County courthouse, DPS, Beaumont Police Department, the jail and the Jefferson County courthouse. If you don't do that by 8, I'm going to have the police seize those generators. It's your decision."

Griffith was frustrated by bureaucratic procedures FEMA was following.

"They tried to tell me we couldn't hook them up until the Corps of Engineers had inspected the sites and decided which generators they would get. I told them, look, you get the generators and our local International Brotherhood of Electrical Workers will hook them up. They wouldn't accept that. They had their own assessment document they had to do and a process to go through," Griffith said.

Griffith assembled a group of law enforcement officers that included the DPS emergency management department, sheriff's deputies from Hardin County that Judge Billy Caraway had sent, and Hardin County Sheriff Ed Cain, who started loading generators.

It was just about then that Gary Jones stepped in.

Jones first met Griffith in the temporary EOC set up in the Elegante' Hotel four days after Rita hit. Griffith had walked up, stuck out his hand and said, "Gary, I don't know you, but we need help."

"We went in and talked and became friends," Jones said.

Although Jones couldn't override orders from his superiors in D.C, he understood why Griffith took such a firm stand on getting generators to first responders.

"I cannot say enough about the leadership of Jefferson County, particularly Judge Griffith. He is a true leader and one of the most compassionate individuals I've ever met. There is no doubt that no only did he care for his citizens and businesses and communities in Jefferson County, but he also cared about his adjoining counties and judges who were dealing with their challenges. A lot of those other judges leaned on Judge Griffith to help guide them."

At 8 p.m. Griffith met with FEMA Logistical Field Supervisor Justin DeMello on the FEMA bus and asked, "What's your decision?" DeMello still said, "No."

Jones stepped in and said he had been able to work out the situation with his superiors at the FEMA headquarters level and obtained permission to release the generators, avoiding an ugly end to the situation. Griffith later learned that Fox News commentator Sean Hannity had speculated whether the judge was going to be arrested for seizing federal property.

"There must have been some media there while I was talking to FEMA because the word got out everywhere," Griffith said.

Before Rita, the agreement between the State of Texas and the federal government stated that prior to a federal emergency declaration, the state would be responsible for generators, said Ted Maddry, statewide procurement manager for the Texas Building & Procurement Commission in Austin. The U.S. Army Corps of Engineers was required to send estimators to evaluate the infrastructure to see what size and type of generator was required, depending on damages.

The policy of the Corps of Engineers evaluation is not a FEMA requirement, but an engineering requirement, said Col. Christopher Sallese, Commander of the Galveston District, which covers 50,000 square miles from Beaumont to Brownsville.

"If your facility needs 800 megawatts of power, I don't want to send you a 50 megawatt generator. So what we had during Rita was a contingent from the 249th engineering battalion that sent 20 soldiers who worked out of Ford Park going to each facility and doing power assessments. Once they had the power assessment, they would bring it back, and we would match that assessment to a generator in the yard. The contractor who has the power contract would load that generator up to go do the installation."

Why couldn't someone simply pick up a generator and install it themselves?

"There were multiple entities that showed up there and said, we want a generator. Give us a generator. That was not how the function was set up to work. The function was if you need a generator we will provide you a generator, and we will come and hook it up for you, and we will provide you the right generator based on an expert analysis of the power requirement you need. And then there was a maintenance piece to that where the contractor has a responsibility to provide a maintenance package and to provide fuel. So when that generator goes into operation, you have one person who installs it, and the contractor has maintenance people who go from generator to generator to make sure things are running right, check the fluid levels and make sure the generators are fueled. The goal is to make that a program where you provide power, and people don't have to worry about maintenance operations for that power," Sallese said.

Safety is a big factor, he added.

"You saw it when people bought personal generators and put them in the garage and a family dies of carbon monoxide poisoning. Or the house burns down because the generator was improperly installed. Who responds to that? The first responders are already tasked to the max trying to take care of the disaster. Now they have these other things that are occurring.

"What FEMA was trying to do was say we will provide you power and come and set it up right so that nobody gets hurt and you don't have to worry about maintaining it and by the way, you don't get more than what you need because we need that bigger generator somewhere else. When you have someone who has a requirement for 50 megawatts and you give them 100 megawatts, the generator doesn't work right. It burns more fuel and doesn't function the way it's supposed to. It needs that load. That's why it is important to size the generator properly from a function and maintenance aspect. I think the rules FEMA had in place were there for public safety. I don't think anybody was trying to make the process any more difficult than it already was," Sallese said.

"We are an 'I want it and I need it now' kind of society. Believe me, that's what we try to deliver. But there are a lot of variables out there. There are places where we tried to send generators and we literally could not get the trucks down the road because of debris. In some cases, debris removal had to occur first so we could get generators in. I think everybody who was there that day was trying to respond in the most expeditious manner possible, but it's a challenging environment.

Estimators usually aren't from the area and don't know their way around the rural roads and woods, adding to the time needed for the evaluations.

"Evaluations are made on the scene and then brought back. Two days later, they will order a generator, and then they've got the logistics of transportation. All we could do is respond to Griffith's requirement verbally and pass it on to the Corps of Engineers. They would make the contact and make an onsite survey and get the wheels rolling. You're talking three to four days to get the generator on site," Maddry said.

"And no," Maddry added, "That's not acceptable. But it's also not acceptable for the cell phone towers to be blown down and cell phone communications to be impaired. But we know that that happens. Normal communication was impossible."

If he were to make an excuse for the slow distribution of generators, Maddry said, it was this: "It was a first time event for people involved. They learned from that."

At the time, FEMA pre-packaged generators in two configurations: a 50 pack and a 100 pack, according to Sallese. Most of the generators pre-positioned in the region already had been deployed to Katrina. FEMA emptied out all the generators in its yard and began purchasing more.

"The generators we had to respond to the Beaumont crisis were actually brand-new generators that had never been used before," Sallese said. "FEMA put them at a FEMA reserve in Ft Worth, where they normally stay and get maintained. They were moved to Reliant Stadium (in Houston) and then to Ford Park."

One of the initiatives the state undertook after Hurricane Rita was requiring city and county governments to do their part to be prepared, something which undeniably was lacking before Rita. Part of that is having power assessments made, something that should have already been in place before Rita.

While county judges aren't expected to know the power requirements for essential services, the county emergency management coordinators should, Sallese said.

"I don't think they understood the dynamics of all the work that had to happen to get a generator in the right place. Should they have known it? Probably not. But a county emergency management coordinator should have known what the requirements were and what was needed. Assessments can come from emergency responders and county emergency officials."

Having pre-assessments done made a big difference during Hurricane Ike, Sallese said, allowing the Corps to respond much more quickly.

FEMA focused on encouraging emergency facilities, law enforcement departments, fire departments and hospitals to implement redundant power. Redundant power means having backup generators in the event of a power grid failure. That, along with redundant power at privately-owned fuel stations, would have made much more fuel available after the hurricane.

"There were gas stations with fuel, but they didn't have power," Jones said. "The big generators cost around $50,000. Most of the stations couldn't afford that, especially when they wouldn't use it every year."

Today, FEMA is working on educating the public about the individual efforts and partnerships that are necessary for preparation and recovery. That includes state and local governments, volunteers, the private sector and faith-based organizations. The campaign calls on the public to better prepare themselves and their families in case a disaster hits.

It's known as the "whole of community," concept, Jones said, and FEMA Administrator Craig Fugate is pushing the educational initiative as a way to help the public understand its role in being prepared for a storm. At its heart, it's a call for personal responsibility.

"You are going to see a lot more public outreach pushing that concept. It's going to take the entire team to make that happen, particularly at the local level," he said, "to make sure families and individuals better prepare themselves in case they come in harm's way and understand the importance of taking care of themselves during that first 72 hours, which is critical."

Don't just depend on government, whether it's state, local or federal, to come in and help, Jones added. "You need to help yourselves in advance through being prepared. It's just common sense."

FEMA also is working to make sure it provides a quicker response to disasters when recovery is beyond the capability of local and state governments, Jones said.

While FEMA took the heaviest criticism during Rita recovery, those who worked closest with the late Chief Jack Colley regard him with respect for the way he treated Southeast Texans. In an interview quoted in the Texas Emergency Management DIGEST, Winter 2006, Colley put the nation on alert to how generously Texans, including Southeast Texans, had responded to Katrina evacuees. It also alluded to the severity of Rita, earning Colley a place in the hearts of many.

"Texas absolutely went the extra mile in their efforts to help our neighbors from Louisiana, Mississippi and Alabama after Katrina. Then Mother Nature decided to mess with Texas and put absolutely every emergency management system, every plan, every first responder to the test," Colley said. "Texas' first responders, state agencies, volunteer groups, cities and communities stepped up to the challenge and performed heroically during Katrina. With Rita, we went into overdrive."

Griffith was among those criticizing FEMA at the time.

"I didn't fully understand the process then," Griffith said. "Looking at Katrina, it seemed that FEMA was the bad guy. Of course, I can't address what happened there. But once I saw how it works and what little staff is funded for FEMA by the U.S. Government and how much they have to rely on contractors, I realized it's the way the government set them up. It's not FEMA's fault. Without what they did with what they had, and with the state emergency management office, we would never have been able to come back as quickly.

"With the number of disasters that had been happening in the last several years, it was impossible for FEMA to meet all the people's needs because of the lack of funding and personnel to do those jobs. That's something very few people understand. Still, with all of that said, I could call Gary Jones and he would get things done on the federal level and I could call Jack Colley and he would get things done on the state level."

Six years after Hurricane Rita, Jones remains complimentary about the efforts he saw in Southeast Texas and the people who made them.

"Judge Griffith will always be one of my heroes. The same with Jack Colley. A lot of bonded true friendships come out of these types of disasters. And I'll cherish those memories, even though they were tough. That's part of this job. I'm proud to have served beside all those leaders and first responders I met during Katrina and Rita. I hope we don't have to go through it again even though we know, if you look at the top ten most costly disasters, that the Gulf Coast is a magnet for hurricanes.

We've got to be ready. The better prepared you are, the better you are going to perform."

"In my lifetime," Jones said, "I'll never forget it."

Chapter Fifteen

Emotional Toll

Perhaps no one knows more about how trauma can affect first responders than Sally Walden, director of network services at Spindletop MHMR in Beaumont. The licensed marriage and family therapist volunteers as clinical director for the Southeast Texas Critical Incident Stress Management Team, which works with emergency responders to deal with their stress after a traumatic incident.

"It could be anything from finding a dead child in a fire to police officers involved in shootings. That team is primarily made up of emergency responders, so they were all on duty 24/7 working during Hurricanes Katrina and Rita. They never got to leave."

During Katrina, Walden provided debriefing and disaster counseling for evacuees, aided by MHMR staff and local counselors from the community who volunteered their time. The stories coming out of Katrina were horrific and heart-wrenching, the kind of thing that requires delicate handling. There was little opportunity for that in the massive shelter, so Walden helped set up a counseling booth and private areas for individual sessions. She remembers counseling one woman who gripped her husband's hand during the flood, only to have the water rip his hand from hers and pull him to his death.

Her group remained at the shelter until the center closed down in advance of Rita.

When Rita hit, Walden worked with the Department of State Health Services in Austin to secure a grant to set up a disaster counseling center. She hired a staff of 20 whose sole purpose was to canvass neighborhoods searching for people affected by the hurricane and let them know what resources were available. Even 18 months after the event, they found people with high levels of depression, anxiety and grief.

"They weren't going to call us and say, 'I think I might need counseling.' It took people going through every neighborhood and knocking on doors and leaving flyers and talking to church groups to identify those people," Walden explained. "A family member might tell us, 'My brother has not left his house in two months, and he's got a problem. Maybe you could go to him.'"

Rather than wait for a suicide or shooting from someone stressed beyond their capability by the storm and its disruption of their lives, Walden's staff moved in after immediate needs, like food, water and a roof over their heads had been addressed.

"Making sure the mental health needs are taken care of is as important a part of recovery as getting blue roofs on people's houses. Mental health needs are critical, too, but it tends to be put on the lower priority. People underestimate how much that kind of prolonged stress can impact people and families. Then you end up dealing with depression and suicide and drug abuse and alcoholism years later – all those things people turn to as unhealthy coping mechanisms."

Walden's team provided mental health first aid counseling and linked clients to the resources they needed.

"For some it was 'I'm feeling overwhelmed because I don't have a place to live.' For others it was 'I need help finding out how I can get my FEMA check.' Others were suicidal."

Walden's CISM team suffered the same damages, losses and stress as other victims, but they put their problems aside to help others. It was months later before the exhausted first responders had a chance to talk about their own losses.

"Everybody was affected. They were in the middle of it all – and none of them left except for the mental health people because they are required to be with the clients. The first responders were doing their jobs. They couldn't have been pulled away to do a debriefing if they wanted to. They were working around-the-clock shifts for a long time."

Emergency responders as a whole tend to put themselves low on the priority list, she said. They didn't have the luxury of time needed to do what therapists recommend: take time off, exercise, eat right, talk with someone.

"They were working around the clock and were lucky if they got a day off for three or four weeks. They were dealing with all the same things everybody else was dealing with. Their homes were damaged; they had trees through their roofs. They had to clean out their freezers. Their families were dispersed. Their number one priority is to take care of public safety and respond to disastrous things. It's asking a lot of people."

Trauma comes with the job for first responders. They learn to debrief each other, talking with someone who knows exactly what they face and how they feel. And they share certain personalities. Most first responders are adrenalin junkies.

"Ninety percent of their time is spent bored and 10 percent is sheer terror – and not a whole lot in between. As a coping mechanism, they all tend to have that sick sense of gallows humor, which is why they tend to socialize with each other. People go, 'Oh my gosh, you can't make a joke about that.' But when they are around their own kind, yeah, they absolutely know what you are talking about. You see it all. You get it. You understand what others see and have to deal with. Journalists are the same way. I think journalists who go to traumatic scenes should get debriefed. Nobody helps them cope with that trauma."

Some emergency responders are able to compartmentalize things and take that situation and put it in a box and not let it filter into their lives, but they are the minority, she believes.

"Even though they would probably tell you that they can separate all that, and they can handle it and not let it affect them, firefighters, police officers and other people who deal with traumatic events have a higher rate of divorce and of substance abuse – unless they have good coping mechanisms. Sometimes their coping mechanisms are not healthy. I know personally that several of them went through marital problems. Some drank too much. Some took it in stride as part of the job and did what needed to be done. But I think it took a toll on everybody, as far as stress level. Their fuse got shorter for things that would not normally faze them. This can be generalized to all emergency service people."

When it comes to evaluating – and judging – how people in public office and others responsible for the citizens of a community perform,

Walden believes in looking at the total situation to gain perspective.

"Some people are able to step up to the plate and thrive on dealing with chaotic, difficult, challenging circumstances. Other people just don't manage that as well. They need structure and routine. It does tend to bring out people who look at things and think of a creative way to cope. I don't think it means some people are any less heroic than others. It doesn't mean anything less about them. It just means we have different personalities. Thank goodness. Because if we were all the same, we'd have everyone trying to jump to the front and be in charge, and then we'd have no one in the parade behind.

"My analogy is you have to have somebody deciding where the railroad is going who gets out in front. Then you have people behind them laying down tracks. You have some people who take direction. There was Guy Goodson and Carl Griffith out in front making the connections and doing things – and you have other people who are worker bees coming in behind and doing whatever it takes to make things happen and following directions. That's good. That's how society works."

It's hard to ask a society in pain not to resort to finger pointing.

"It's human nature to look for somebody to blame. To me, it doesn't provide any value. To me, and this is from a therapist's perspective, it doesn't help in therapy to evaluate what kind of mother your mother was or what happened in your childhood. It helps to evaluate where you are, where you need to go and how you are going to get there. To spend a lot of time blaming and trying to assess fault is wasted time. If you can use that time to be productive and move yourself forward, that's where things get better.

"There is going to be anger, and it is normal to feel resentment and grief and all those things people went through, especially with Katrina, when they lost homes or family members and weren't able to get rescued off the bridge. There were some pissed off people in Ford Arena after Katrina. There were a couple of times it was really scary. And you can't deny people those emotions, but you have to try to redirect that into something more productive than staying in that angry, hostile place. Some had some very legitimate complaints. However, spending the next three months being angry doesn't help move them past the event and forward in their lives."

What is productive is to review the traumatic event and ask, "What will we do next time? How will we avoid that situation? How will we manage logistical things in a different way?"

"That's the way to make a disaster make more sense. Take what you've learned and improve things," Walden said. "It makes you feel like you have a little more control than sitting around waiting for the next bad thing to happen, and you've not done anything to prepare."

Six years after Hurricane Rita disrupted the routine Anne Huff had built for the daughter she traveled to China to adopt, the aftereffects linger.

As chief training officer for the Beaumont Fire Department, Huff couldn't simply pack up and leave with her family when Rita headed her way. The department sent Huff to the emergency operations center in Port Arthur to help with evacuation plans. Huff got a call from her daughter's day care.

"She's 3 years old at the time. She's throwing up and has fever – and I can't go to her. So I called a friend and asked if she could please go pick Katie up because I couldn't leave right then."

Huff's two sisters, their children and pets, and her elderly mother and father had made plans to evacuate from their homes in Galveston, where the storm was predicted to hit. They stayed at Huff's home. When Rita changed courses, they had to pack up and evacuate a second time with Katie.

As her family worked to escape the hurricane, Huff had to stay focused on the tasks at hand at the EOC. She didn't have the luxury of outing her family first. Instead, she was working to secure the safety of the citizens she had sworn to protect.

"My mother had health problems, and my sister had called me from the road and said they were stuck in traffic that had backed up and the car was overheating, and my mom wasn't doing so well. I was worried about her. And about that time, we saw the magnitude of the storm on the screen, and I really thought there was a good chance we were going to be just .. gone."

Huff told her sisters how much they meant to her and said, "Make sure Katie knows I love her."

"At that point in time, I thought there was a good chance I might die because the storm looked so big and so bad. To me, it looked way worse than Katrina looked. That got a little emotional for a minute, but then I had to get back to my job."

Katie had to endure not only the separation from her mother, but also the arduous trip to safety. She knew her grandmother was sick and heard the stressful conversations.

"They thought there was a good chance my mother might die in the car. My daughter saw all that. I was separated from my daughter for three weeks. When my sisters, who work at University of Texas Medical Branch, had to go back to work, I had to fly Katie to my brother's home in South Texas. So she's getting booted around because I'm at work."

Katie went through more than a child should, Huff said, and she still is not over the trauma. The little girl who had traveled all the way from China to find a family was extremely well adjusted. From day one she slept in her own bed, safe and secure.

"Now, she is afraid of the dark and will not sleep in her own bed. She's terribly afraid of something happening to me. When we've had other mandatory evacuations, I've made arrangements for her to leave. She is afraid I am going to die. It's so sad."

Others who had to put their personal lives aside to fulfill their duties also felt the stress. For many, it was a cumulative effect felt long after the storm had passed.

"I did not realize the emotion and toll that the hurricane took on me until I saw my family many weeks later. I looked tired and lost several pounds during the hurricane recovery. Loss of sleep, poor diet, and loss of weight were effects that we all experienced," Shawn Oubre said.

Look at a photo of Mark Blanton before the storm and one two years after, and you'll see a different man.

"The hurricane aged me more than anything in my entire career – and several people have told me that. I was a baby-faced guy even at 48. Now I look like an old man. Deputy Chief John Owens and I worked 54 hours without sleep. It was hard to keep up with the long hours, the frustration of not being able to get supplies, and dealing with food issues. My men and women who work for me were expected to do patrols and take care of others, and yet they also were victims. Many of my officers lost their homes. I lost my home. It was totaled. Here you are, you've got 12 on and 12 off and you can't even go take care of your own."

The post-hurricane stress soon surfaced, Blanton said, and became a morale issue. More than anything, he said, he worried about his department.

"The long hours with no days off, the fatigue, the inability to take care of their own, and seeing such devastation took its toll. When they finally get off and can go to their own homes, they are too tired to go try to salvage anything because they have to be back on the job 12 hours later. A lot of my people actually worked 22 hours before they got any time off. Owens and I worked 54 hours at one stretch. That has affected my health more than anything in my whole life."

Watching his men and women work under such circumstances cemented Blanton's pride in his department.

"I had one dispatcher who failed to respond. All my officers all did their duty. I am very proud of them."

Blanton said the hurricane changed his life in many ways, not only from the stress of meeting his responsibilities while looking out for the safety of his officers and the community, but from a more personal perspective.

"To this day, six years later, I still sleep only a few hours, and then I'm up. I never sleep more than four hours. Your sleep pattern is disrupted because you go so many hours without sleep. Sometimes, after working 54 hours, if there was an opportunity for a 30-minute nap, you took it. Because of sleep deprivation, towards the end, I started to get concerned about making sure I was making clear decisions. People tell me about orders I barked that I don't even remember. I know that we did it, but I don't remember giving that order."

For Ingrid Homes, having to do her job while feeling isolated was stressful. She already was exhausted from monitoring the health needs of Katrina evacuees.

"Then Rita hit us. We just didn't know what to do and that was more a mental attitude. We knew what we needed to do, but just the thought that we were in this building and the windows were blowing out was scary. I was walking across the street and my glasses were blown off my face, and I couldn't catch them. The wind was still high. Most stressful was the thought that my family was gone, and I was the only one here. Some of those things were just a little overwhelming. It's a high level of responsibility and leadership is necessary. You can't show that you are as devastated as the people you are serving."

In hindsight, Holmes believes a professional psychological de-briefing after Katrina would have helped tremendously.

"I think we never got over what we saw those people go through. I really would have done something differently for myself – and my staff – to just take us down some from Katrina before we faced Rita."

While Southeast Texans were struggling to get a handle on what had happened to their homes and communities, people as little as an hour's drive away were going on with life, something that was hard for Brit Featherston to reconcile.

"The fifth day after the storm I decided I was going to meet my wife and kids in Houston. They had come back from San Antonio to Houston and were staying at a friend's house. We met at Goode Company Bar-B-Q, and I couldn't sit still. It was so irritating to see people acting normal. They had no problems whatsoever. They are eating barbecue, and 80 miles away people can't flush their toilets and don't have air-conditioning. Why don't these people realize there are people in despair in Beaumont? I stayed overnight, and then I just had to get back."

Sometimes, it took the people around them to step in and help first responders. For Owens, that came from the U.S. Forest Service.

"They were a Godsend. They would actually shadow me. When they saw that I would stay up three days sometimes without sleeping and got to where sometimes I wouldn't make any sense, they would say, John, you need to go rest. We've got this. And my assistant coordinator at the time, Wayne Roccaforte, would take over. I'd take a nap, and they would keep me informed. They were trained to understand and recognize what we were doing and assist us in giving advice with moral and psychological support. They could do this, in part, because they weren't victims."

During interviews with National Public Radio and several television stations, Owens spoke up for his team.

"I told them that people forget that we are charged with unbelievable responsibility, which we readily accept in regards to disaster management and subsequent recovery, but we are also victims too. We have wives and children and homes and pets and valuables and all the stuff everybody else is dealing with. But we have to put ourselves aside – and you can do that, but it's still in the back of your mind.

"I'll give you an example. My wife and her mother initially went to Wildwood with a relative. After the storm, she called me panicking. 'John, there's trees down everywhere. We're stuck. There are six families up here, and we are marooned.'"

Psychologically, Owens said, that was always in the back of his mind.

"My wife is with her mother, who was 81, and they are there with no electricity, no water, and the miserable heat. She is calling me, crying, wanting to know what to do. People don't understand that. You have to prioritize and put your personal life aside. And some people couldn't do that. They just could not do it."

Brit Featherston was one of many who noted that despite the stress, numerous people were able to move past their own problems and rise to the occasion.

"You never know what kind of community you live in until you have something like this happens. There were so many unsung heroes who will never be known. They did what needed to be done without regard to credit or attention or notoriety. They took care of folks. It was pretty remarkable."

Five years after Rita put his team to the test, Port Arthur Police Chief Blanton's voice turns bitter over how it often seemed that those who had responded en mass to the plight of Hurricane Katrina's victims turned their backs on the victims of Rita.

"Major Owens called me from a hurricane conference he attended in Florida in 2006. The director of the national hurricane center at the time made the comment that Rita made landfall in a sparsely populated, insignificant part of the country. Major Owens and I both took great offense to that. Just look at what Hurricane Ike later did to this insignificant area and what it did to oil prices. We are not insignificant."

After Owens approached the director and told him how the statement made him feel, the director apologized for his comments, saying he was referring to densely populated areas such as Houston.

"He was very sincere in his apology and made a public statement later in the conference, clarifying his statement," Owens said.

Blanton also didn't take kindly to the choices for speakers at a presentation on Hurricane Rita at the International Association of Chiefs of Police, of which he had been a member for decades. The conference was supposed to be a recap of what happened before, during and after Rita, as well as what law enforcement learned from it. The first presenter was from Lake Charles, which had been hit hard. Blanton could respect that choice. It was the second presenter than got his dander up.

"It was someone from the New Jersey State Police. What does the New Jersey State Police have to do with a hurricane on the Gulf Coast? I sent a letter to the IACP telling them I would no longer be a member. I told them, "I cannot believe that you had people in Jefferson County, Port Arthur and Beaumont who had experienced Rita and you're going to have someone else teach a seminar on what to do in a hurricane."

Blanton never received a response.

Chapter Sixteen

Good Samaritans

In the dark days after Hurricane Rita blew in, citizens and leaders alike fought against falling into despair over losses that seemed insurmountable. Business owners wondered if they would be able to reopen. Workers wondered if they still would have a job. Home-owners despaired that the houses they had worked so hard for were severely damaged.

Among the heroes of Hurricane Rita are the non-profit organizations, committed industry partners, dedicated civic leaders and faith-based organizations that heeded the call to love their neighbors as themselves, proving once again the unfailing generosity of the human spirit.

Beaumonter Angela Baker answered a call from the United Methodist Committee on Relief (UMCOR), the not-for-profit global humanitarian aid organization of the United Methodist Church. UMCOR responds to natural or civil disasters that are of such magnitude that they overwhelm a community's ability to recover on its own.

Baker met with UMC Bishop Janice Riggle Huie, along with local churches, who wanted to put together a team to respond to families without insurance, the elderly, single parents, disabled and those without other means of help.

"We decided to put an office together, organize a staff, and train volunteers to meet with families and get the necessary paperwork filled out," Baker said. "We needed someone to set up the construction department, someone who would set up bringing teams in and housing them, and someone to handle accounting. We set up a website and needed someone to manage the database. We had to hire supervisors to help with the family advocates. From Nov. 1, 2005 to March 2006, we put the entire staff together and got volunteers lined up for Spring Break and got the ball rolling."

The first group, mainly college students, began work in January 2006, staying in damaged churches.

"The churches in Southeast Texas opened their doors, and they were in the middle of the disaster. We had our offices in three churches at no cost to us. All of the churches of all denominations let volunteers sleep on their floors and fed them and took water out to them in the heat," Baker said.

The group focused first on Jefferson, Hardin, Chambers and Orange counties. All of the volunteers were from outside the area, Baker said. Later, retired people and church groups who travel wherever there is a disaster joined in. Close to 80 percent came from outside Southeast Texas. After the area began to recover, local people joined in. Methodists began the program but were joined by numerous denominations and people of other faiths, Baker said.

"The majority were Methodist only because of our connected system when word gets out. We had Habitat for Humanity, Presbyterians, who have a huge disaster program; Baptists, Catholic Charities, Mennonites, Church of Christ, Disciples of Christ, Jehovah's Witnesses – I learned so much about other denominations. We were repairing homes using the funds this group managed to put together. Government aid did not come down until two years after Rita, at least, not in helping the people we helped – uninsured and underinsured."

Methodists sent out a plea around the world and raised $4.8 million for Rita recovery. That money was "from the pews," Baker said.

"It was a huge response. One of the things I'm very proud of as an organization is the fact that we raised about a million and a half on top of that through teams who came down and saw what we were doing. They would go back to their churches and tell them what a great experience it was and we would get checks in the mail.

"The State of Texas Governor's Office received money from corporations after Rita. They sent us money that was given to counties for unmet needs. We got $338,000 for Jefferson County and $92,000 for Orange County. Catholic Charities gave us $25,000 in gift cards for supplies. It was amazing how this all came together. We got $265,000 from the Southeast Texas Emergency Relief Fund. People would come repair homes and then leave the tools and equipment for us. A church in Ohio mailed us gift cards to Lowe's and Home Depot so we could buy what we needed."

Altogether, a total of 10,000 volunteers with 804 teams from 38 states and Canada completed 929 homes, saving $7.5 million in labor costs.

"I know without a doubt that the recovery efforts would not have advanced as quickly without the work of the faith-based organizations. And, for the first time, faith-based had a voice in Austin and Washington," Baker said. "We formed an alliance and spoke about the slow response and the lack of funds. We fought to get the resources for Southeast Texas that were needed. I learned so much about the way government works in a disaster – slowly.

"It was eye-opening in so many ways, but the blessings outweighed the frustrations. There were so many 'God moments,' and I know that He was the real leader. Our construction coordinator came to us from South Carolina. He heard from someone who heard from someone... Our accounting person had recently moved here from Wisconsin. Our volunteer coordinator was a member of Christ Covenant Church and did an amazing job of hospitality – lodging and meals. Our family advocate managers were three women who had never done this before. They came to the first meeting and said what can we do? A Lamar intern had never built a website before but put ours together so we would have a database of people and skills."

Baker said the experience was "the most rewarding thing I've ever done in my life. It changed my life and made me more compassionate about the needs of others and made me truly understand what mission work is all about. I am in awe of people who do that."

The UMCOR team shut down operations on July 31, 2010.

"It was hard to close the door and walk away – but I don't want another hurricane," Baker said.

Rev. Harland Merriam of St. Andrews Presbyterian, co-chair of the Southeast Texas Interfaith Organization (SIDRO), was instrumental in their success, Baker said. SIDRO is made up of various faith communities, businesses and community organizations. Joe Higgs, organizer for the Gulf Coast Interfaith organization based in the Houston and Galveston area, was the co-chair.

"I met Joe Higgs a week after Hurricane Rita," Baker said. "He walked in and was looking around. He had somehow managed to get here and wanted to help. From there, a week later, Joe was at Harland's church and the first meeting took place. We had those meetings every Thursday for two years at St. Andrews. It was Joe and Harland that put all of this together to form the organization. Harland, who is a chaplain in the U.S. Army, used those skills to get people ready. He was great."

Another vital organization after the hurricane was the Salvation Army.

The Salvation Army is an international, evangelical part of the universal Christian church with a message based on the Bible and motivated by the love of God, said Judy Kelfstrom, development director for Salvation Army in Beaumont.

"William Booth founded the Salvation Army in 1865. We came to Beaumont during the Spindletop Oil Boom in January 1901 and have been actively working to meet human need without discrimination ever since," Kelfstrom said.

During Rita, the Salvation Army was one of, if not the first, relief organizations on the scene. When reviewing the notes she made after Katrina and Rita, Kelfstrom realized every entry was about trying to do the most good with their time, talents and treasures.

"People are truly giving by nature and yet most don't know how to give during a disaster. The Salvation Army, with its long standing reputation of being first on the scene to minister to those in harm's way, was the vehicle many used to say 'Here am I, how can I help, use me.' We stand ready to meet those challenges whenever and wherever they may occur," she said.

From Sept. 23, 2005 to Oct. 30, 2005, Salvation Army canteens served more than 410,000 hot meals, and volunteers donated more than 21,000 hours of service to hurricane victims and emergency responders. They were on the ground serving meals the day after the storm.

"The Salvation Army has always been a tremendous first responder. We were there on the street serving the next day," said Beaumonter John Reaud, who was chairman of the board of the Salvation Army during Rita's strike.

For Rita, Salvation Army joined forces with another faith-based group, the Southern Baptist Texas Convention. The two teams work in tandem to pool their resources. The SBTC Disaster Relief Strike Force set up a kitchen at Ford Park, where Salvation Army had mobile canteens in place.

Southern Baptists are believed to be the third-largest disaster relief operation in the country behind the American Red Cross and The Salvation Army, with more than 30,000 trained volunteers available to respond to national emergencies.

The Salvation Army provided food and the Baptist teams prepared it, using canoe paddles to stir food in 30 to 50-gallon kettles. The Salvation Army then took the food to their canteens to feed relief workers and local residents. The Southeast Texas Food Bank and the Houston Food Bank provided food boxes to the Salvation Army, while the government provided food commodities and bulk supplies.

The Huntsman Corporation long has been known for its charitable works. Jon Huntsman, owner of Huntsman Chemical Corporation, as it was known at the time of Rita, had a very personal connection to Rita recovery on three levels. First, his family upbringing and value system call him to help those in need. Second, his faith is committed to outreach ministries worldwide. And third, he has a huge base of employees and friends in Southeast Texas.

Huntsman's company bought Texaco Chemical Co, which has assets all over Texas and around the world, mostly in Jefferson County, primarily Port Arthur and Port Neches.

"Huntsman had hundreds of millions of dollars of assets in that area and across the border in Lake Charles," Huntsman said. "Shortly after Katrina, the Church of Jesus Christ of Latter Day Saints had a major regional welfare center to take care of the emergency needs mostly of the LDS people, but over the last few years the church has changed dramatically and now keeps supplies for people of all faiths and backgrounds."

As it did for Katrina victims in Mississippi and Louisiana, the church brought in blankets, sleeping bags, clothing and other supplies after Rita.

A week and half before Rita, Huntsman and senior church officials flew to Southeast Texas in his private jet.

"I wanted them to see what the church had done and the supplies we provided in Jefferson County to Judge Griffith at the makeshift accommodations at Ford Park. So I took Boyd Packer, president of the 12 apostles; David Burton, presiding bishop over welfare assistance, Russell Ballard and several others. We had Judge Griffith take us through what had happened after Katrina and how we could better supplement any further hurricane relief out of our site near Houston. How could we be first on the spot to be as helpful as possible as a church?"

The group spent all day with Griffith and John Reaud, brother of Beaumont attorney and philanthropist Wayne Reaud.

"John was working at Ford Park as a Salvation Army director there with the Reaud Foundation. Wayne is on our board of directors and a dear and close friend. He set up all the meetings for us. John and Carl took us around and showed us what Katrina had done to Jefferson County. When Rita came, which was a great shock, we had just taken that tour. I knew the area well and the people. Rita bypassed us in Mississippi and New Orleans and hit head on in Beaumont and Jefferson County. It absolutely devastated our business there and created havoc for six to eight months. In some cases, it was several years before we were able to bring back some of the facilities we had purchased from Texaco Chemical and that we had built in the Jefferson County area," Huntsman said.

When the church knew the storm was headed toward Jefferson County, they activated its LDS welfare center out of Houston. The center brought in 5,000 gallons of much-needed gasoline, as well as 60 to 70 truck loads of bedding and large quantities of food.

"We were able to distribute it where we had been just a few weeks before, which is ironic," Huntsman said. "At that time, I was on the national board of the American Red Cross, so I knew something about disasters through that. Clearly we were in early because we were anticipating another potential hurricane and had told our folks there in the Houston center to be prepared to leave immediately if anything should happen. Because we were only a few hours away, we were able to get there quickly even with so much damage to the roads and airport."

Huntsman Corporation placed a priority on helping employees with temporary housing. Their refineries had taken a big hit, sustaining extensive damage from the winds and flooding.

Rita was the "most ferocious storm to plow into the petrochemical industry in Jefferson County," Huntsman said. For some, it took months to recover. For those with major damage, it would be two to three years.

"It took us a long time just to get our employees' homes and lives in order, which we addressed first. We had insurance claims up until a year and half ago from Rita. It took that long to complete rebuilding certain parts of our site," Huntsman said.

Huntsman's family has provided $2 billion in relief through the years in the U.S. and around the world, such as aid for the devastating floods in

Thailand and Haiti, as well as earthquake, fire, flood and storm recovery in the States.

"We have a 23-year history, and I've been grateful to be a part of that. I do it because I believe it is the right thing to do. As an asset, my faith is very helpful. I've been blessed immensely with a large fortune and I believe that fortune is best served in helping other people."

While it seemed the rest of the world knew little and cared less about the magnitude of recovery needed after Hurricane Rita, Huntsman makes it clear he saw what was done regionally by so many to help their neighbors.

"Being on the board of the American Red Cross in Washington and being a member of their executive committee, I've seen virtually all of the crises we've had in the last 10 years around the United States – and I've never seen a better operated crisis management facility and leadership as that Judge Griffith gave Beaumont. That clearly had to help the city immensely in handling the devastation and then recovery. I could not think more highly of the judge. He was a terrific field general, the best I've ever seen. He was surely the commander in chief of that area and knew how to delegate extremely well.

"The organization he had put together in Jefferson County was by far better organized than any other in the Gulf Coast region that I saw. People knew what to do, where to go, how to handle things, who was in charge, the role of the Red Cross and what happens when the churches would come in. He saved not only many lives, but calmed the waters immensely. He should get a lot of credit for this because he clearly orchestrated what must go down in history as one of the finest management operations in this kind of an emergency situation ever seen in any city. And he did it in a very professional manner."

One of the hard-working groups that fought for financial aid for the region is the Southeast Texas Emergency Relief Fund (SETERF). The plan began with a meeting between Judge Griffith and Beaumont Attorney and Philanthropist Regina Rogers.

After Rita, individuals and groups began calling Griffith wanting to donate money. Rogers was the first to offer aid.

"I remember telling Carl I wanted to make a contribution to help the victims. He said, 'Regina, the need is so great. We have to help these people.'"

Rogers told Griffith she would call businessman Joe Penland, whom she greatly respected. Rogers and Penland, co-founders of the fund, each put in $25,000 to get things started. Penland gave interviews at Ford Park about the fund, imploring the public to join their efforts.

Griffith and Kathleen Jackson of ExxonMobil thought the fund should be set up as a 5013c non-profit organization. ExxonMobil would need that designation before it could make a substantial donation.

"Carl was the conduit for them for the fund," Rogers said.

Rogers enlisted the help of Baptist Minister Mark Viator, whose background includes public affairs. He brought in other ministers.

"Mark is a motivational speaker and was able to gather some momentum. He marshaled the troops and helped direct the funds to organizations where there was very little administrative cost and the money would go to the people who needed it most."

Rogers called on her relationships with people across the country to get funds, including George Irish of the New York City based Hearst Corporation, which owns the Beaumont Enterprise. Irish helped spread the word through the company's newspapers. She enlisted the Houston-based law offices of Bracewell & Guiliani to fight to bring attention to the group in D.C.

"We knew we needed to add some influence in Washington and it was important that we were represented there. We knew there was a lot of competition for funds for hurricane relief, and we were in last place. Mississippi, for example, had a large presence and influence. We knew we had to make a strong case. We didn't want our residents to be forgotten. Our skilled lobbyists helped us present the case in a very forceful and effective way," Rogers said.

The group reached out to everyone it could to raise funds.

"We were successful in part because there were so many people involved. We met frequently, coming together in a meaningful way to help literally thousand of residents impacted severely by the storm. It's a real testimony not only to people of different religious backgrounds, but residents of different regions who were very involved," Rogers said. "I was relieved and inspired by the cooperation between so many different counties. It wasn't that each one was interested only in their county. They realized it was for the good of everyone in Southeast Texas."

SETERF provided money for victims of Hurricanes Katrina, Rita and Ike. After Rita, the organization gave $3 million to victims through gift cards, support of community social service agencies and short-term loans.

Some of the largest contributions came from Motiva ($1.5 million);

ExxonMobil ($1.25 million); BASF ($289,000); Meadows Foundation
($250,000); Houston Homebuilder Bob Perry ($100,000); Wilton P.
and Effie Mae Hebert Foundation ($100,000); Flint Hills Resources,
($100,000); AmeriCares ($50,000); Capitol County Mutual Fire Insurance Company ($50,000); H-E-B ($50,000); Marathon Oil ($50,000);
BP ($50,000); Gene and Jerry Jones (Dallas Cowboys) Family Charity
($50,000); and the Bob and Janice McNair (Houston Texans) Foundation
($50,000).

The Greater Beaumont Chamber of Commerce is one group that appreciated what SETERF had been able to accomplish.

"Every year across the country, there are disaster everywhere. But
what happened with Katrina and Rita on top of each other is there was a
historical demand for small business loans, which are part of the federal
government's response," said Jim Rich, president of the chamber. "At
one point they had 5,000 applications. In November, two months after
Rita, the Small Business Administration had to hire 3,000 people just to
handle the volume of loans. They were overwhelmed. Nobody was going to get any money soon – and that was not counting Texas. That was
Mississippi, Alabama and Louisiana. If you had a disaster tomorrow, you
could probably get a loan in 10 to 15 days. They were taking six months."

The chamber created its own loan program to bridge the gap,
beginning with $1 million from the Texas Emergency Relief Fund and
$200,000 from SETERF.

"We had $1.2 million. It had never been done before. There was no
program and no criteria in place. We had to go lobby to get the money.
We wrote up a grant that we literally had to make up," Rich said. "It
wasn't like we could go to somewhere else in the country and say, how
do you do this? We are proud that we put that all together and were able
to help small businesses in the six counties we serve. This was not meant
to do anything but bridge the gap between getting an SBA loan or getting reimbursed by insurance."

When people from other parts of the country heard about the fund,
they began calling the chamber. One example was Cedar Rapids, Iowa,
which had extensive flooding.

"The lobbying to get federal funds appropriated to the area took four
or five attempts. It wasn't until the fifth appropriation from the disaster
that Texas got any real money from Congress. To get to that point, we
really had to be visible and argue about the forgotten storm. We were
able to get national attention on follow-up stories from the Washington

Post and the New York Times. We hired two sets of lobbyists. Regina Rogers is an unsung hero there because she funded the money for one group and paid the first two months of their fee. And then we hired another group so we had both Democrats and Republicans covered."

Like Rogers, Rich was pleased with the cooperative spirit he observed.

"We went to Washington united, recognizing that you can't go as Beaumont or Port Arthur. We had to go as an entire region, and we had to be fairly specific on what we were asking for," Rich said. "We also discovered that Southwest Louisiana had the same problem in that they weren't getting much attention for Rita in their state because of the impact of Katrina. We ended up going together on some things that continue to this day. I go to D.C. every May with representatives from Southwest Louisiana. We didn't even know each other before Rita, and now we have some solid relationships and call on legislators together because of Rita. Southwest Louisiana and Southeast Texas have a lot in common. Rita helped open that up."

Other important assistance came from the Texas Workforce Commission, the state agency responsible for unemployment benefits.

When Hurricane Katrina hit, TWC employees were spread about the state, primarily in Southeast Texas and Houston, said Larry Temple, director of TWC in Austin.

"Our people were working with national emergency grants for people affected by the storm. A month later, we got our own personal storm, Rita, and those who were serving people from one hurricane all of a sudden became victims themselves. I think that brought a level of empathy no one had ever seen before. It was pretty amazing. We had people who didn't have homes and with family members who had lost everything, and they were working to help other people find jobs."

TWC became a communication hotline for people who came to their trailers to file for FEMA assistance, unemployment, and to communicate with family and friends using TWC's Internet and phone access at two different locations, said Diane Rath. At the time, Rath was chair and commissioner representing the public. She resigned in March 2008 to become vice-president of ResCare Workforce Services, headquartered in Louisville, Ky, but still lives in San Antonio.

"TWC had started moving from a paper-based office system in 2001, and it very much assisted those impacted by Rita because we didn't have offices that were inundated and didn't have paper files like Louisiana did.

Everything was electronic on the Internet," Rath said. "We immediately went to work to be on site as soon as possible after the storm to allow people to file for unemployment so they can get cash. When the storm hits and businesses close, paychecks stop. You have immediate cessation of cash flow right when people need it desperately."

Temple said the group's Southeast Texas Board was well prepared and had a good disaster plan.

"They were able to muster back after the storm. In addition, the neighboring 27 workforce boards around the state as well as our own employees did an hour and a half commute to help people. It was a team effort."

Temple and one of his staffers drove to Beaumont, using emergency credentials to get in. It was a ghost town, he said. He found Griffith, whom he had worked with during Katrina, walked up to him and said, "I have about $84 million and need to get $26 million to you and your mayors. Can we talk?"

Luckily, Temple had arrived at the tail end of a press conference, he said, and Griffith dropped everything to talk with him.

"The great thing about these emergency grants is individuals who were out of work were able to be employed locally with cleanup. A lot of that labor and some equipment were funded by these grants. We were able to pull down additional child care dollars and dollars for employment training."

TWC ran into the same issues that others had – the lack of equal treatment for the victims of Rita.

"The Katrina relief that was virtually mandated went above and beyond the state. When we got our own relief for Rita, it was the standard emergency grant without all the bells and whistles of Katrina. We weren't able to do for our people what we did for Louisiana. We worked with our congressional delegation and the U.S. Department of Labor and got it amended so we had parity to serve our people affected by Rita. Katrina had gotten so much national publicity and so much response that no one thought about Rita. So we were happy to get some parity," Temple said.

Rath also felt the frustration of trying to get maximum relief for the people of Texas.

"Rita truly was the forgotten storm. We had a million people coming in the state of Texas from Louisiana and then we get hit with our own storm coming, but no one wants to hear about it because everyone is still focused on the tragedy of New Orleans. We're dealing with relocating these people and our roads, which normally are clogged with people trying to escape the storm, are already clogged with relocating Katrina refugees. We had to prepare for another storm which would impact Texas and Texans directly. We were still providing service to Katrina people, so we had a double whammy as a state."

TWC was able to serve 14,986 Rita-affected customers; 864 were employed in temporary disaster relief; 14,349 received core services such as help with resumes and aiding employers looking for workers as well as workers looking for employment. They provided 5,490 intensive services, such as comprehensive employment testing and counseling; 875 received training services.

"We got a waiver for a small business capitalization program for training and business development training. We gave $5,000 to each of the 310 small businesses. And we worked 64,235 claims for unemployment in those 22 counties impacted by Rita," Temple said. "It was an exciting time. I tell you, it was pretty hectic and pretty scary with the magnitude of the services needed down there. It was very gratifying, and also an honor to, as an individual and part of a state agency, to see the faces of the people you helped. It was so personal. One of the best things that came out of all of this is I made a real good friend in Carl Griffith, and anyone who knows Carl knows that's a plus."

Rath, who covered many storms in her 12 years with TWC, said she saw tremendous commitment and leadership in a local area with the attitude of "We pull up our boots and take care of our own."

"But because Texas was still dealing with the effects of Katrina, our resources as a state were stretched very thin. It took a great deal of regional and community leadership to be able to respond to the damages of Rita. I'm very proud of what they did in Southeast Texas. I'm pleased we were able to provide a little bit of help to them during that time," Rath said.

The Hurricane Katrina supplemental bill spearheaded by Sen. Kay Bailey Hutchison in the Senate and Rep. Kevin Brady in the House of Representatives finally brought parity to Texas for Rita recovery. Passed on June 15, 2006, the Emergency Supplemental Appropriations Act for Defense, the Global War on Terror, and Hurricane Recovery 2006 secured $428.7 million in emergency funding.

Louisiana Sen. Mary Landrieu, who had fought hard for the people of Louisiana who endured not only Hurricane Katrina but Rita as well, played a key role in securing the money.

"Mary Landrieu agreed to support my bill because she didn't believe it was fair either," Hutchison said. "That really helped. Getting equity for one state in a bill is very difficult, but we did it because it was just egregious. Those counties would never have been able to pay 25 percent of the huge cleanup costs."

Yes, Texans wanted parity, but they understood that their Louisiana neighbors had endured unbelievable losses, both in life and property. They opened their homes and hearts to do what they could for the evacuees. It never was a competition; it was about seeking equality from the federal government.

The names of the two major hurricanes of 2005 will forever be linked. When officials from FEMA and the State of Texas talk about the damages, resources needed, and aftereffects, it is "Katrina/Rita," as if they were one.

The two storms shared funds and resources and came so close together they seemed inseparable.

Not to the people of Southeast Texas and Southwest Louisiana.

As Texans know, Louisiana suffered some of the worst damage from Rita. Sen. Landrieu wrote this in a letter commemorating the fourth anniversary of Rita:

"Four years ago today, Hurricane Rita came crashing ashore along the Louisiana/Texas border. With winds in excess of 120 miles per hour pushing a 20-foot wall of water, the storm wreaked catastrophic damage across Southwest Louisiana. The storm at its peak was the most intense ever to have entered the Gulf of Mexico, breaking a record set only three weeks earlier by Hurricane Katrina. When the skies cleared, Rita ranked as the third-most-expensive natural disaster in U.S. history.

"Hurricane Rita caused 120 deaths and billions of dollars in damages to the Gulf Coast. Whole communities – including Hackberry, Cameron, Creole, Grand Chenier, Holly Beach, and Johnson Bayou – were almost completely destroyed.

"Despite the devastation, the people of Southwest Louisiana have come together determined not only to rebuild their communities back to the way they were before this ferocious storm, but to make them stronger. This unyielding spirit is at the heart of the core values that make me so proud to have helped their efforts."

Epilogue

Time will pass. Memories will fade. A new generation will become complacent. It will be harder for emergency coordinators and those who try to protect us to make us heed the warnings. My hope is that this book not only will tell the rest of the country what happened here, but will serve as a reminder to any community in harm's way – including our own - how important it is to be prepared.

We dodged a bullet because we were afraid – and we got out of harm's way. If Rita had not weakened somewhat before she came ashore, this story might have reflected a very different experience.

While acknowledging the lives shortened by the trauma of evacuation, the lives of the five who died of carbon monoxide poisoning in Beaumont, and the tragic bus wreck that killed nursing home residents as they fled from Rita, it is clear that when it came to fatalities, our preparation, evacuation and response provided as good an outcome as was humanly possible.

Had the images of Katrina not been so raw in our consciousness, had we not feared the same fate might await us, had we no forward-thinking leaders and fast-reacting first responders - we might have been the ones on TV.

If it comes down to having others acknowledge what happened here – or having images like those of Katrina flashed across the nation - we'll choose anonymity.

Hurricane Rita Timeline

Monday, Aug. 9
- *Katrina makes landfall near New Orleans*

Friday, Sept. 16
- *Ford Park emptied of Katrina evacuees and closes as shelter*

Saturday, Sept. 17
- *Workers begin cleanup at Ford Park*
- *Tropical depression forms east of the Turks and Caicos Islands*

Sunday, Sept. 18
- *18th tropical depression of the season signals Rita's formation*

Monday, Sept. 19
- *Rita becomes hurricane*
- *EOC opens at U.S. Coast Guard Marine Safety Unit in Port Arthur*

Tuesday, Sept. 20
- *Rita hits Florida Keys*
- *Texas officials establish joint Federal/State/Local operations center in Austin*
- *Priority given to evacuating Louisiana residents and high-risk Gulf Coast communities*
- *Sabine Pass calls evacuation*

Wednesday, Sept. 21
- *Rita upgraded to Category 4*
- *National Weather Service predicts landfall near Galveston*
- *Texas requests immediate return of all assets deployed to Louisiana*
- *Department of Homeland Security Secretary Chertoff appoints Coast Guard Rear Admiral Larry Hereth as Principal Federal Officer for FEMA*

Thursday, Sept. 22
- *Rita becomes Category 5 with 175 mph winds*
- *Mandatory evacuation ordered for Houston and Galveston*
- *Mandatory evacuation ordered for Jefferson County*
- *FEMA deploys 11 National Disaster Medical Teams & 14 Urban Search and Rescue teams to Texas*
- *FEMA & Department of Defense pre-stage water, ice, food, tarps and generators in Louisiana and Texas*
- *Jefferson County Schools closed*
- *Evacuation of Medical/Special Needs citizens begins at 8 a.m.*

Friday, Sept. 23
- *Rita drops to strong Category 3*
- *Coastal storm surge 15 feet above normal*
- *Coast Guard ordered to evacuate*
- *Jefferson County EOC moves to Edison Plaza in Beaumont*
- *Hurricane Rita makes landfall in Southeast Texas/Southwest Louisiana*
- *After the Storm*

Saturday, Sept. 24
- *EOC loses power at 1:30 a.m.*

Sunday, Sept. 25
- *Beaumont initiates dusk to dawn curfew; Local State of Disaster declared for Jefferson County*
- *Entergy outages peak at 286,609*

Wednesday, Sept. 28
- *EOC moves from Edison Plaza to the MCM Elegante Hotel*

Thursday, Sept. 29
- *Points of Distributions (PODS) open at Parkdale Mall, Central Mall, and the Ford Park baseball fields*

Friday, Sept. 30
- *Jefferson County reopened from 7 a.m. – 7 p.m. to allow citizens to assess damage*
- *Water service restored, but still unsafe for consumption*

Saturday, Oct. 1
- *PODS now include Gateway shopping center, Blue Bonnet Park, Memorial High School, and Labelle/Fannett Volunteer Fire Department*
- *Nederland City Hall opens from 8 a.m. – 6 p.m.*

Sunday, Oct. 2
- *Christus St. Elizabeth, Renaissance Hospital, and Southeast Texas Regional Medical Center operational*

Monday, Oct. 3
- *Garbage service resumes in Nederland*
- *V.A. Mobile Medical Unit set up in Beaumont to treat veterans only; Jefferson County establishes citizen hotline to take calls from 8 a.m. – midnight; boil water notification lifted for the City of Beaumont*

Tuesday, Oct. 4
- *50% of power outages restored*
- *Postal service resumes in Port Arthur*

Thursday, Oct. 6
- *Garbage services resume in Beaumont*
- *Boil water notification lifted for the City of Nederland*

Friday, Oct. 7
- *Richardson evacuees return (first bus of evacuees to return)*
- *Boil water notification lifted for the City of Groves*

Saturday, Oct. 8
- *Boil water notification lifted for the City of Port Neches*

Sunday, Oct. 9
- *Boil water notification lifted for the community of Central Gardens in Mid-County*

Monday, Oct. 10
- *90% of power outages restored*
- *Beaumont Independent School District reopens*
- *Mandatory evacuation lifted for Jefferson County*
- *Curfew lifted for Beaumont*
- *Jefferson County employees urged to return to work*

Tuesday, Oct. 11
- *City Council meetings resume; Jefferson County opens residential debris drop-off locations*

Saturday, Oct. 15
- *Taiwan Buddhist Tzu Chi Foundation makes donation and presentation to first responders*

Monday, Oct. 17
- *Port Arthur, Nederland, Port Neches-Groves Independent School Districts reopen*
- *Lamar State College Port Arthur resumes classes*
- *Beaumont municipal bus system resumes routes*
- *Nutrition and Services for Seniors resume meal delivery*

Acknowledgments

You don't spend 18 months working on a book of this scope without help.

First, thanks to former Jefferson County Judge Carl Griffith, who often remarked that the resourceful, dedicated, and humble heroes of Hurricane Rita deserved to have their stories told – and that I should consider writing a book honoring them. Rita truly was the forgotten storm, and no one is more proud of the first responders and others who came to our aid than the Judge. Many of the interviews conducted for this book would not have been possible without his endorsement to officials who would have paid little attention to a request from a retired journalist from Southeast Texas.

Heartfelt thanks to Beth Gallaspy for her fine editing skills. For 20 years, you have been a blessing in my career and personal life.

When it comes to heroes, my family has been mine during the writing of this book. My husband, Joel; daughter, Stephanie; son, Christopher; daughter by marriage, Sheila; and grandsons Jordan and Jarrod turned down many an invitation or went without me during the crunch of deadline pressure. No one could have a more supportive family. All gave valuable input to various aspects of the book.

My thanks to all those who spent many an hour with me, sharing their recollections, providing documents, calling others on my behalf, double-checking facts, giving me additional time as I triple-checked those facts, and providing photographs they took before, during and after the storm. They tell the story well.

Thanks also to those who played a role in acquiring information, providing leads, reading behind me, etc. (including Gloria Prince and Gene Soper). You know who you are and know how grateful I am.

And thanks to the Pediment team, who published this book – and made sure Hurricane Rita's Heroes will not be forgotten.

Our Family and Rita

While we lost huge 100-year-old pecan and cedar trees and our beautiful old magnolia was badly damaged, we considered ourselves blessed. We might have lost fences and had a hole in our roof and carport, but we didn't lose our home, as so many did during Hurricane Rita. Our daughter, Stephanie, also had damage, but her home survived. Like many others, our son, Chris, was blocked in his home by fallen trees and had to cut his way out with a chain saw to go help his grandparents and other neighbors.